Atlantic Edge

WEST CORNWALL

Written by **Des Hannigan**

Editor **Mike Foxley**

Contents

Editing & concept   **Mike Foxley**
Written by   **Des Hannigan**
Creative direction & design   **David Kingsnorth**
Print production   **Design & Print**

Photographic contributors

Liam Addison	**Bob Berry**
Simon Cook	**Ander Gunn**
Tim Guthrie	**Des Hannigan**
Rob Jewell	**Ian Kingsnorth**
Joe Lewis	**Steve Martin**
Charles Mason-Smith	**Ashley Peters**
Andrew Ray	**Adam Sharpe**
Philip Trevennen	**Paul Watts**

Penwith District Council and Des Hannigan have made every effort to ensure the accuracy of the information contained in this publication, but accept no responsibility for any errors or misrepresentation.

ISBN 978-0-905375-09-0

Published by: Marketing and Communications Office,
Penwith District Council,
St Clare, Penzance, Cornwall, TR18 3QW.
www.penwith.gov.uk

Printed using environmentally friendly paper and inks.

Cover photograph
The Crowns, Botallack.
Ander Gunn.

Back cover photograph
Bosulval, Newmill.
Ander Gunn.

Left
Atlantic Edge.
Bob Berry.

West Cornwall has long been recognised as having one of the most beautiful landscapes in the world. It is a landscape that is given exceptional emphasis by the sea and by brilliant light and colour. This landscape is also exceptional because of its underlying geology and structure and in the way in which it has been used throughout history. The surviving relics of prehistory that lie scattered across the moorland hills and along the clifftops constitute one of the finest archaeological resources in Europe. The old tin and copper mining area of St Just and Pendeen, with its dramatic ruins and artefacts, has won the highest accolade of all by being designated as part of a World Heritage Site. The St Ives Tate Gallery, Penzance's Penlee House Gallery, the Newlyn Gallery and numerous small private galleries now reflect the area's international standing as a centre of excellence in art and craft. The reputation of West Cornwall as a tourism destination is second to none and tourism in the area seems likely to flourish even more as a sustainable and rewarding industry. For many years Penwith District Council, in partnership with town and parish councils, environmental bodies, community organisations and local people, has worked ceaselessly and fruitfully to nurture and promote this outstanding Cornish heritage area, not only through local democracy, essential services, tourism and the promotion of community interests, but for its own sake as a beautiful and historic landscape. In this book, *Atlantic Edge*, all the strands of the remarkable story of this exceptional Cornish landscape are brought together through evocative and informative writing and outstanding photography. It is a privilege to have been involved in its preparation.

Mike Foxley
Marketing and Communications Officer
Penwith District Council

Penwith District Council

Foreword

by Kurt Jackson

The Penwith district of West Cornwall is unique.

The name translates from the Cornish language as the last place, the place at the end, the final district. This geographical isolation is one reason for its uniqueness. Penwith has retained its distinctiveness, but has had to keep its self-reliance. In doing so it has maintained a strong sense of community.
That uniqueness and sense of community have been captured beautifully by the outstanding photography and the evocative text of Atlantic Edge.

When I go out of my front door and climb on top of the hedge I gaze over a patchwork of tiny fields, known locally as quillets and mowhays, down to the Atlantic cliffs. When I go out of my back door and climb on to the moor I am on the backbone of Penwith; heather, gorse, rock, big skies and over 270 degrees of sea and skyline.

Land use in Penwith is non-intensive. There is still a natural resonance about the landscape.
We are talking about signs of the past all around; we are talking about clarity of light; and always about the rock. The granite is never far away, pushing through the earth, enclosing the fields, holding the roofs up above our heads. From this has risen a whole host of clichés both pictorial and written; the ancient landscape, the pagan sites, the tin mine against the sunset over the sea, the aquamarine waters, the Atlantic surf; but they are true, they do exist and are the daily realities of life in Penwith.

Is this why there are so many of us here? The painters, writers, makers of one sort or another, all trying to circumscribe these clichés and to come to terms with all this Penwithian information; to comprehend, absorb, maybe disseminate, but finally use it all creatively.

What a joy it is to be so far West, to be immersed in a community that is so dominated and steered by this edginess, this land by the sea, this near island, this closeness to the almost primeval feel of the landscape; No matter where you go in Penwith you are never more than a few miles from a town. Yet, everywhere feels wild, with nature still in charge; the changing Atlantic weather, the light, the rock – all maintain this exhilarating feeling of isolation and emptiness.

Penwith is unique...

Kurt Jackson
St Just, September 2006.

Opposite page
*Kurt Jackson painting on
the cliffs at Botallack.*

Above
Getting closer; dusk.
Kurt Jackson.
February 2002.
Mixed media.
560mm x 585mm.

Introduction

People look with longing to the west, to the Atlantic edge of Cornwall especially, the first and last foothold of Island Britain.

Richard Carew's description of Cornwall as a demi-island in an island fits more precisely the area described in this book; that final rocky peninsula of West Cornwall that thrusts into the Atlantic from between the great bights of St Ives Bay and Mount's Bay to terminate sensationally at the granite-beaked promontory of Land's End. The neck of land between the two bays is only four miles wide. The peninsula measures only nine miles at its widest point. It is barely sixteen miles long. Its coastline, from St Ives to Penzance, measures thirty-six miles. This dramatic knuckle of land lies within the regional area of West Cornwall. Its historic and administrative name is Penwith, 'the far end'. Its topographical name is the Land's End Peninsula.

This book celebrates, with words and photographs, the drama and beauty of West Cornwall's Atlantic edge. It sets out to explain why the area is so distinctive and so different to the rest of Britain, and to the rest of Cornwall, by describing its topography and geology and by looking at how ancient people shaped many of the landscape features that still exist. It explains why the area has earned so many awards and protective designations for its heritage and its landscape value.

The Land's End Peninsula is bounded by a dramatic coastline of high cliffs and rocky promontories, a vertical mosaic of bare rock and dense vegetation breached only where narrow valleys reach the sea and where bays are lined by beaches of golden sand. There are no tidal creeks or wide river mouths along this savage coastline. The sea is not overshadowed by high mountains and long, subsidiary peninsulas, such as you find on the west coasts of Ireland and Scotland. The West Cornwall coastline is so sharply defined and dramatic that the sea dominates everything and is rarely muted. It seems to merge seamlessly with the sky. The impression of great distance and of spaciousness thus generated is exhilarating and liberating.

On the peninsula's north coast, between the towns of St Ives and St Just, a narrow strip of fields separates the edge of the coastal cliffs and the rock-studded flanks of moorland hills. The original pattern of these fields is delineated by granite walls, or 'hedges' as they are known in Cornwall, those gloriously un-English bulwarks of rough stone that enclose a core of earth crowned with turf. The fields date from pre-Roman times and their survival and their continuous use from that period make them unique.

The north coast of the Land's End Peninsula has place names that resonate with ancient grace notes; Wicca, Zennor, Morvah, St Just, Sennen. These are the human settlements. The rocky hills, headlands and offshore rocks match them with their refrain; Rosewall, Boswednack, Zawn Duel, Carn Galver, Bosigran, Manankas, Kenidjack, Maen Dower.

From the rocky summits of the coastal hills, the land descends gently to the south across tangled moorland towards the lusher shores of Mounts Bay. The moorland is peppered with the tombs, stone circles and standing stones of the Bronze Age, and by the broken walls of Iron Age hill forts and the dimpled remains of Iron Age houses. Over one thousand prehistoric sites have been identified within the area; a total that makes the Land's End Peninsula the most richly endowed archaeological landscape in Britain.

These ancient remains have survived because they are built of enduring granite. They are a sparse collection, however, relative to the huge number of

Left
'...the sea...is rarely muted'.
Bob Berry.

similar sites that probably existed in ancient times. Many of these sites were damaged because of the rapacious enthusiasm of 19th century 'antiquarians' who were looking for valuable grave objects such as pottery and metalware. Local people took the broken slabs and smaller stones of the scattered sites and used them to build barns, houses and roads. Yet, the very durability and weightiness of granite and the hardness of the ground on which the ancient remains lie, meant that something substantial survived into our time. This same granite has ensured the survival of the artefacts and ruined buildings of the copper and tin mining industry that have made their own dramatic impact on most of Cornwall's north coast.

The central and southern parts of the Land's End Peninsula are made up of fields and woods dotted with low-roofed houses and cottages, clustered farmsteads, hamlets and villages, all set within a network of sunken lanes and granite hedges. The few main roads are convenient without being intrusive and within this carefully managed landscape, farming, that most ancient of Cornish industries, still flourishes.

The Land's End Peninsula has no great rivers; but brisk streams from the high ground have cut long valleys to the south and shorter courses to the north. Encircling the peninsula is Carew's 'besieging' ocean from which generations of Cornish people have sought a living and upon which they founded a powerful tradition of seagoing that sustains the hard-pressed but still vigorous West Cornwall fishing industry of today.

The ancient people who built stone circles and burial chambers were not self-conscious artists; but they produced artefacts that by their nature alone were beautiful, as well as functional. Their landscape was peppered with boulders and rock outcrops that had been sculpted into dramatic shapes by permafrost, wind and water. Their world was flooded with luminous colours and with a brilliant light that was intensified by the mirror of the sea. Their skies were vast canvases of colour and form. All of these elements are with us still and they make the Land's End Peninsula an ideal workplace for artists of all disciplines. In West Cornwall today, painters, potters, sculptors and other craftspeople sustain a creative industry that is as significant today as the region's older industries were in their heydays. West Cornwall is famous in the international Art world. The Tate Gallery, St Ives, Penzance's Penlee House Gallery, and the Newlyn Gallery are the main centres of Cornish Art and, together with a vibrant network of smaller public and private galleries, craft shops and studios, they play a major part in Tourism, a leading industry of our times.

Penzance and St Ives are the main towns of the peninsula. Newlyn, Hayle, Marazion, and St Just are smaller centres. A score of villages and hamlets completes the pattern of rural settlement. The peninsula has a population of about 63,000 people. In summer that total is increased by huge numbers of visitors who are drawn to the area by their longing for the west and by the peninsula's beautiful landscape, its beaches, its historical sites, its Art, and its charming and hospitable local people.

"People look with longing to the west, to the Atlantic edge of Cornwall especially, the first and last foothold of Island Britain"

Left
...'Their world was flooded with luminous colour...'
Joe Lewis.

The Fragile Earth

The Fragile Earth

"Although there is a feeling of tremendous space, the landscape is really minuscule. Even the smallest of changes stands out a mile."

Patrick Heron. *Painter.*

Granite is the dominant exposed rock of the Land's End Peninsula. Its colour, texture and sculpted shapes make it beautiful to look at. It is famously 'golden' in the sun as if its ancient heat still lingers. Generations of sculptors and painters have been inspired by the patterns of its weathered surface and by its random yet aesthetically pleasing forms. The more ancient killas slate, into which the granite intruded, is darkly coloured and chaotic in its form. Yet it too is beautiful.

Sunsets are spectacular on this Atlantic edge. On clear summer evenings there is a rust-red glow that momentarily suffuses the landscape as the sun, flushed with refracted light, sinks below the horizon. Yet mist and fog can blur the landscape. It can seem threatening when storm clouds move in from the west and when huge waves that begin in mid-Atlantic crash to a shattering halt against the cliffs. The wind blows at will, fresh and breezy beneath bright blue skies or fierce and rain-sodden from the vast open mouth of the ocean.

The landscape endures. It seems unchanging in its forms. Yet the coastline and the moors, the wild country of the Land's End Peninsula that we see as being 'unique', 'beautiful', 'haunting' and 'natural' are, in part, the creation of thousands of years of human influence and exploitation. There are few sections of the West Cornwall coastline that people have not exploited, for survival's sake or for profit and pleasure. The wilderness of old was fair game for work and waste. The first miners, the 'old men' as they are called, delved into the cliff faces and slopes of the coast in search of ore. At the foot of dripping cliffs, rusting iron bolts and wedges still nestle in cracks and fissures; the twisted remnants of metal

ladders hang from the rock.

Ledges were chipped out of cliff faces and rough shelters were erected wherever a small boat could be worked profitably from the shoreline. The smugglers of the 18th and 19th centuries used remote landing places. Farmers and smallholders excavated trenches and tunnels through low cliffs; they gouged out tracks across rocky foreshores so that seaweed could be gathered for use as fertiliser on coastal fields and on tiny meadows known as quillets. The great cliffs were seen as convenient launch pads from which to tumble rubbish into the sea; out of sight and out of mind. In the days when coal fires kept coastguards warm, below every coastguard lookout there was an 'Ash Can Gully'; a convenient rubbish chute. Each year until the war of 1914-18 coastguards poured gallons of whitewash down the golden granite slabs at the seaward end of the great cliff of Bosigran on the peninsula's north coast. The cliff was four kilometres from Pendeen Lighthouse and when the whitewashed mark on the cliff was obscured by fog, the lighthouse keepers knew that it was time to sound the foghorn. The safety of seagoers meant more in those days than the aesthetics of landscape. Today you would risk being arrested for such cavalier treatment of a now cherished 'environment'.

In the 19th century, parts of the Land's End Peninsula's north coast were industrialised by tin and copper mining. The physical and visual impact on the landscape was damaging and at times devastating. The industry operated in a Victorian world in which there was scant concern for the welfare of those who worked in the mines and even less for the damage done to the wild landscape. Profit overwhelmed the picturesque when it came to Victorian enterprise.

Today, the redundant mining landscape of West Cornwall is a valuable archaeological resource of world significance. The cliff tunnels and rocky landing places of an earlier age are cherished as being part of an admired tradition. The edges of sea cliffs are

protected as precious biological *refugia*, the last resorts of plants, lichens, birds, insects and mammals that have been driven from their inland habitats by modern farming methods. All has become 'heritage', to be protected, conserved and cherished. And rightly so; but the historical ironies are worth acknowledging.

Despite this pressure on the landscape, the hard ground of the Land's End Peninsula has resisted much of the wear and tear of human intrusion. Before the machine, and outside the mining areas, the effect of human activity on the landscape went with the grain of the land and merged with it. Rocky ground and smallness of scale meant that much of the peninsula was spared the most damaging effects of industrial agriculture. Clearance of ancient field hedges to create larger, more easily managed units did take place on some farms during the latter half of the

20th century, but the practice has now ended. Thus, for most of the 20th century the farmed landscape of Penwith escaped the worst effects of the modernisation that has transformed so many parts of rural Britain into featureless, bland countryside. The landscape of Penwith is recognised as being worthy of preservation because so much of its historical features have survived.

Such recognition is long established. The Land's End Peninsula was included as part of the proposed Cornwall Coast National Park recommended by the 1947 Dower Report of the National Parks Committee. National Park status was not awarded, but in 1959 most of the peninsula was designated by the Countryside Commission as being part of the *Cornwall Area of Outstanding Natural Beauty*. The entire coastline was defined as a Countryside Commission Heritage Coast by 1986. Long stretches of the

Above
Carn Galver Mine, Bosigran, near Gurnard's Head.
Simon Cook.

Opposite page – top
St Just.
Simon Cook.

Opposite bottom – bottom
Cornish Hedge.
Simon Cook.

"Penwith escaped the worst effects of the modernisation that has transformed so many parts of rural Britain"

coastline are *Sites of Special Scientific Interest*. Cornwall County Council's Structure Plan recognises parts of the area as being of *Great Historic Value*, *Great Scientific Value* and *Great Landscape Value*. The peninsula is within a *Tourism Restraint Area*. The farmed landscape of the northern half of the peninsula was considered to be of such archaeological and biological importance that it was designated in 1987 as an *Environmentally Sensitive Area*. The ESA scheme devoted funds to promoting conservation-minded farming under the control of the then Ministry of Agriculture, Fisheries and Food. The mining landscape of the peninsula's north coast along with the mining areas of Devon, mid-Cornwall and North Cornwall has been designated by UNESCO as being a *World Heritage Site*, perhaps the highest accolade of all.

Such designations are richly deserved. They acknowledge not only West Cornwall's scenic beauty, but also its importance in geological, biological and archaeological terms; the richness under the skin. The designations may lose their impact when referred to by such acronyms as *AONB, CCHA, SSSI,* and *WHS,* and the litany of designations can make your ears ring. But they are crucial to the continuing survival of West Cornwall's living landscape, not simply as picture postcard scenery, but as a biological whole.

Beautiful landscapes are vulnerable and their fabric is often tightly stretched. Farming more than any other activity has shaped the landscape of the Land's End Peninsula and it is to the farming practices of prehistory that we owe the mosaic of tiny fields and interlocking stone hedges that are such a memorable feature of the area today. For centuries, the landscape bent farmers to its will, yet at the same time it satisfied their needs. The rocky ground was best suited to animal husbandry and the land was mainly under a grazing regime that ensured some balance with the natural environment. Farmers made their living from small-scale, mixed farming within a local market economy. It was a way of life that remained unchanged for generations until the 19th century when dairying, with mainly Guernsey herds, emerged as the main farming activity.

Such specialisation demanded increased effort and efficiency. It led also to the decline of mixed farming and crop rotation. During the 20th century the practice of keeping cattle under cover in winter led to an increase in the size of herds. In turn this meant that more grass was needed for converting to silage with which to feed the overwintering cattle. To meet the need many fields were used exclusively for the growing of grass. In turn this encouraged farmers to remove intervening stone hedges so as to merge small fields into larger more easily managed units. The use of bigger and more powerful tractors and earth diggers led to the widening of gateways and field lanes and to the uprooting of 'whaleback boulders'. These are the smooth, silver-grey tops of huge granite rocks that protrude from grassy fields and that previous generations of farmers tolerated as obstacles to cultivation. Many sunken lanes became overgrown and impassable through disuse. The payment of subsidies for breaking in unused land encouraged the cultivation of areas of moorland. Technology and economics seemed about to overpower the ancient landscape.

By the 1980s perceived damage to the landscape by farm mechanisation and expansion was evident. The problem was structural and was a side effect of economics and technology. Farmers are vulnerable to

Top
Overwintering cattle.
Ian Kingsnorth.

Middle
Daffodil pickers.
Ashley Peters.

Bottom
Silage – cut and dried.
Des Hannigan.

Right
Meadows at Botallack.
Simon Cook.

the pressures and bewildering changes of a modern economy that leaves little room for choice. They embrace new technology that improves their working practices and increases their profits. This is a timeless human response to the advantages of technology and does not reflect modern attitudes only. It is not entirely fanciful to imagine that the Bronze Age builders of the great quoits would have welcomed the assistance of a modern mechanical digger that could accomplish in a few hours their back-breaking work of several months.

The Environmentally Sensitive Area scheme was introduced to the north coast of the Land's End Peninsula in 1987. The take-up by local farmers was high compared with ESAs in other parts of the country. Unsympathetic change was thus stemmed in the West Cornwall ESA without handicapping a still robust farming industry that would eventually face other less easily solved problems. The ESA scheme helped to throw a protective mantle over the unique landscape of West Cornwall's northern coast and

moors. Good environmental practice is reflected in the planning policies of Cornwall County Council and of Penwith District Council, the local authority responsible for the Land's End Peninsula. Planning policies on new buildings in the landscape, on the conversion of redundant rural buildings and on rural development generally, give favourable emphasis to landscape and Nature conservation. Penwith Council is responsible for Heritage Coast management and for other environmental schemes. The council also has a policy aimed at encouraging sustainable tourism and its Tourism Department has generated a number of imaginative projects aimed at maximising visitor satisfaction. These range from recreational use of rural areas to minimising physical impact on the environment.

The National Trust has major landholdings in West Cornwall and has a positive policy of further land acquisition. The Trust owns, and protects, through fruitful conservation work, many of the peninsula's finest coastal features, including Zennor Head and

Zennor Hill, Bosigran, Gurnard's Head, Cape Cornwall, Mayon Cliff at Sennen, Porthcurno Beach and St. Michael`s Mount. It also owns the prominent inland features of Trencrom Hill above Lelant and Chapel Carn Brea above Sennen. Other groups, such as the Cornwall Wildlife Trust and the Cornwall Heritage Trust, own and protect small areas of wild land and are involved in collective initiatives. English Heritage in Cornwall has current responsibility for a number of ancient monuments within the Land's End Peninsula.

As well as the professional bodies that work to protect the West Cornwall landscape there is an important voluntary involvement in conservation by local people, individually and as members of conservation groups. Local schools are involved in environmental initiatives that combine practical work with education.

Preserving the beautiful landscape and rich biology of West Cornwall is thus assured through official designations and the work of a wide range of agencies. In these early years of the twenty-first century there is hope for the future of a landscape, which, by its nature, has preserved so much of the past. An understanding of that past is the next step towards understanding that the West Cornwall landscape is much more than beautiful 'scenery' to be admired for its own sake.

Top
Bosigran, near Morvah.
Des Hannigan.

Left
Mousehole Thrift.
Simon Cook.

Granite Kingdom

Granite Kingdom

William Gilpin belonged to a cultural milieu that favoured the 'picturesque' in art, the representation of an idealised landscape that already looked like a picture, or a painting by such great artists as Claude Lorraine or Poussin.

The eighteenth century taste was for managed landscapes and an iconography of rounded hills and wooded dales dimpled with lakes; the whole fitting neatly into a picture frame. Aficionados even carried small, clear glass lorgnettes through which they peered, while making critical asides, at sections of landscape as they travelled through the countryside. Gilpin and his contemporaries were repelled by nature in the raw. It was not until a later generation of Romantic poets and painters responded with spiritual fervour to the savage grandeur of mountains and of the sea that 'wilderness' became recognised as being beautiful for its own sake.

Today, the granite of West Cornwall may still be 'barren and naked'; but it makes up the good bones that underlie the striking topography of the Land's End Peninsula. The linear jointing system and eroded weaknesses of granite have produced spectacular cuboid towers and buttresses on the great cliffs at Land's End, Gwennap Head and Porthcurno. The same jointing has produced the piled clusters of the moorland tors and coxcomb ridges of Bosigran, Carn Galver and Zennor Hill. Erosion of this remarkable rock has even contributed material and colour to the famously 'golden' sand of the peninsula's silken beaches.

Granite may be the lodestone that gives West Cornwall much of its attractiveness, but a substantial part of the peninsula is composed of other rock types. These may be less photogenic than granite, but they can be even more dramatic visually and more interesting geologically. Too many commentators attach the label 'granite' to most of the peninsula's rock types; but the black-faced cliffs of Tater du, Zennor Head, Gurnard's Head, Pendeen, Kenidjack and Cape Cornwall do not fit the golden cliché. Such cliffs are composed of ancient material, some of which was greatly altered because of its proximity to the intense heat of molten granite that erupted from deep within the earth's crust. The resulting rocks have complex geological names, but are often given the collective name of 'country rock' or the local names of *killas* and blue elvan. *Killas* is an old word for clay slate; elvan means 'spark'.

Millions of years ago, before granite and before almost everything, West Cornwall was an unformed part of the young Earth's fragile crust upon which volcanic storms and violent earth movements created havoc. Four hundred million years ago, during a fifty million year epoch known as the Devonian, layers of sand, silt, mud and pebbles thousands of feet thick were deposited on the bed of a vast ocean that covered the area of what is now South West England. In turn these layers were compressed into harder shale and sandstone and were later disturbed by cataclysmic mountain-building storms that thrust the layers of sediment thousands of feet high. In the West Cornwall of today we walk blithely on the roots of ancient Alps that once extended as far as South West Ireland and Brittany.

After these upheavals, the ancient rocks lay broken and twisted into peaks and troughs. About 280 million years ago, from deep below the scarred and chaotic surface of the region, molten granite erupted into the underbelly of the mountains. The locations of the most powerful eruptions are marked today by the granite masses of Dartmoor, Bodmin Moor, Carnmenellis, the Land's End Peninsula and the Isles of Scilly. The whole of Cornwall has an irregular backbone of granite that plunges deep below ground between the exposed high points; a wriggling dragon's back that runs into the Atlantic.

The word granite derives from the Italian word for 'grained'. It is an igneous rock and the word igneous derives in turn from the Latin for 'fire'. Granite is a hot property in every sense. In its molten state of magma, granite altered greatly the sedimentary rocks amongst which it burst like bombs. The heat was nuclear, the pressure likewise. The softer sedimentary rocks that were in contact with the magma were baked and compressed until they metamorphosed to harder and denser forms. As the magma cooled volatile gases and fluids, associated with the eruptions boiled and sizzled along the network of fissures that had formed in and around the granite. These bubbling intrusions reacted chemically with the surrounding rocks and as they cooled and crystalized they formed mineral lodes including copper, tin, lead, silver, wolfram and zinc. The granite and the veins and sheets of ore lay embedded within the 'aureole', the cap of weaker and looser sedimentary rocks that still covered the domes of granite after the eruptions.

During the following 150 million years this aureole of softer rock was slowly destroyed by earth movements and by the eroding effect of wind and water. The debris from this process spilled out across the lower ground that now makes up the present sea bed. Domes of more resistant granite protruded from sheaths of crumbling metamorphic and sedimentary rock and it is the tougher remnants of these rocks that survive today in the dark-coloured sea cliffs of Penwith's north coast.

For the following sixty-five million years the whole of the south west was submerged periodically beneath shallow seas. When this period ended, geological changes and erosion continued for another 350 million years. Human history is a single breath compared with such immense periods of time. During the periods of long-term submergence the highest parts of Dartmoor and Bodmin Moor appeared as rocky islands, much as the Isles of Scilly appear today. West Cornwall itself, was a submerged landscape. The granite ridge that runs today from Trencrom Hill through Zennor Hill, Carn Galver and on to Chapel Carn Brea above Sennen was an undersea reef. Each time the sea level fell, a wave-cut shelf of land

"The granite ridge that runs today from Trencrom Hill through Zennor Hill, Carn Galver and on to Chapel Carn Brea above Sennen was an undersea reef"

three million years ago. During successive glaciations most of Britain was submerged beneath ice sheets that were up to a mile deep. There is some evidence that at the peak of the final Ice Age, about 12,000 years ago, the tattered frontier of an ice sheet may have reached as far as what is now the North Cornish coast and to what is now the island of St Martin's on the Isles of Scilly. West Cornwall was free of ice, but temperatures were extremely low. Permafrost bit deeply into the ground and closed like a fist round the granite bosses shattering them along their lines of weakness. Its cleaving action produced masses of the loose rock known as 'clitter' that now studs the north coast hills above Zennor and Morvah.

A million years ago the Land's End Peninsula, as we know it, was ready-made. But the familiar topography of today's peninsula was still part of a widespread landmass that incorporated the Isles of Scilly. During the glacial epoch the sea level was over 300 feet lower than it is today. From the present north coast of West Cornwall a rocky shelf extended for several miles towards the icy frontier. It was a landscape unused, utterly pristine in the geological sense, raw and rocky and littered with rubble heaps and with waterlogged basins. The distant sea was still clouded with sand and grit. The site of modern Penzance was probably buried under heaps of rubble

emerged. This has left the Land's End Peninsula with a continuously flat shelf of land immediately behind the edge of its sea cliffs. This 'coastal' shelf once lay beneath the sea. It is narrow along the north coast, between St Ives and Pendeen, but is much wider at Land's End and is at a much lower level along the shores of Mount's Bay.

The Land's End Peninsula was not affected by the glaciation of the Ice Age period that began about

and mud, St Ives likewise. Land's End was an unidentifiable part of a landmass that extended far to the south-west and that was truly 'barren and naked' and was puddled with muddy lakes and meandering streams.

Climate was temperate during inter-glacial periods. Algae developed in the primeval waters; sub-arctic mosses and sedges colonised the basic soils on which wind-borne birch seeds from the warmer south took root. From this time onwards West Cornwall had some form of vegetation, even during the peak periods of successive glaciations. Periodic freezing and thawing of the ground during glacial periods caused a loosening of the earth, which led to the slippage of soil and gravel down hill slopes. This produced the mix of pebbly clay known as 'head' that is found in the stream valleys and along some cliff-

edges of the Land's End Peninsula. Soil also built up on the sea-smoothed ground of the peninsula's coastal shelf. It was during this period that particles of tin and copper were washed down into the valleys to await the work of early tin-streamers thousands of years later.

Sea levels rose substantially between successive Ice Ages, and then fell as the expanding ice caps absorbed huge quantities of sea water. Legacies of this period are the remarkable raised beaches of the Land's End Peninsula, examples of which are seen at Porth Nanven near St Just and along the coast towards Sennen. Raised beaches are a geological 'cake-mix' of sea-polished boulders embedded in a cliff-face of soft clay and topped with rock-studded earth.

The final Ice Age ended by about 8,000 BC; not with a bang, but with prolonged contractions and

occasional resurgence. In time Britain was ice-free. Soon the sea penetrated the low marshy ground between England and France. The desolate, low-lying landscape between West Cornwall and the Isles of Scilly was inundated also and its rocky ridges and pinnacles survive today as undersea reefs. This fabled 'Land of Lyonesse' may have seen desultory movement of primitive Old Stone Age hunters before the flood; but of fantastic cities and tolling bells, wizards and mounted warriors, there were none. The reality is even more fascinating.

Soon after 7,000 BC, warm, dry conditions reached an optimum in West Cornwall. Thickets of hazel, birch, oak and alder stood deeply along the lower ground and extended far out across the boggy plain of what is now Mount's Bay. The site of modern Penzance was a copse of shrubby trees drained by streams that cut deep channels far out across a

coastal plain that is now covered by the waters of Mount's Bay. Trees surrounded St Michael's Mount; the summit of the Mount was rocky and bare; the sea was a distant gleam on the horizon. But the forests of this coastal plain were soon submerged when the sea level rose. Today, the broken remnants of trees, petrified by age, lie buried beneath the sand in Mount's Bay and are exposed occasionally during very low tides and after big storms.

By 5,000 BC the Land's End Peninsula was truly on the Atlantic edge. Even in those ancient times West Cornwall had an enviable climate. Temperatures increased as the drift of warm air from the Gulf Stream edged farther northwards. Winters were brief and mellow, springs and summers were sweeter and warmer than they are today. The glossy leaves of birch, alder, oak and hazel glistened with dew in the clear mornings; a green mantle of moss and lichen covered the woodland floor. Meadowsweet, with its froth of tiny white flowers, was abundant in the open areas as were plants such as scabious and bugle. The beautiful mountain avens, or windflower, was thickly strewn across the high ground. Common weeds such as goosefoot, dock, stinging nettle, and willowherb choked the river valleys. Hazel and oak yielded nuts and acorns and there were blackberries and sloeberries for harvesting.

Through this rich feeding ground, elk, red deer, roe deer and the large wild cattle known as aurochs moved at will. Smaller mammals such as wild pigs, badgers, pine martens, hedgehogs, and even woodmice were abundant. The coastal waters were thick with shellfish. Seals, dolphins, whales and numerous species of fish thronged the offshore waters. Seabirds were plentiful and cranes, lapwings and smaller woodland birds were common on shore. After millions of years of earth building and upheaval, Nature had finished the job with a flourish, but with a gentle hand. Conditions were now ripe for the less selective, less gentle hand of humankind.

Top
Towards Land's End.
Bob Berry.

Left
Chair Ladder Cliff, Gwennap Head, Porthgwarra.
Des Hannigan.

The Unwritten Years

The Unwritten Years

"...it stands black against the summer sky, touched with the pathos of man's handiwork overthrown. On every hand lie cromlech, camp, circle, hut and tumulus of the unwritten years."

Edward Thomas. 1909.

The first people to inhabit Britain were from foreign parts. They were probably hunter-gatherers of the Palaeolithic, (Old Stone Age) period of 200,000 years ago who crossed the marshy land bridge from Europe into southern Britain during more temperate inter-glacial periods. They came to forage through the ice-scarred landscape and to hunt animals that had moved north in search of grazing.

These early immigrants might have wandered across the western landmass from which modern Cornwall emerged, though there is no evidence of this. They had no sense of place. They claimed no local identity. They sheltered beneath the overhanging banks of rivers and in damp and gloomy caves from where they emerged to hunt mammoth and bison. They withdrew for long periods to the warmer south of the European landmass when bitter winds whistled down from the north of Britain in front of the resurgent ice. They left few lasting signs of their presence on a landscape that was then reshaped by glacier, permafrost and knife-edged arctic winds.

About 8,000 BC, soon after the final retreat of the ice, descendants of these Palaeolithic people probably settled permanently in southern England. A few of them reached a notional 'Cornwall' that had evolved into something of an earthly paradise of game-filled woodland and fruitful seas. These hunter-gatherers of the Mesolithic, (Middle Stone Age), moved seasonally between the foreshore and the higher ground. They ate shellfish, gleaned food from the abundant plant life and hunted game. Again, it is not certain that they settled for extended periods in West Cornwall, though evidence of their vestigial hearths and flint-chipping sites have been found at

Gwithian near Hayle, Kenidjack near St Just, and in the St Buryan area.

A Neolithic, 'New Stone Age', culture emerged in West Cornwall by about 4,000 BC. It was shaped by gradual changes in the Mesolithic hunter-gatherer life style and by the spread of technological changes via individuals and communities. It was unlikely that there was a sudden influx or invasion of immigrants with a ready-made culture of their own. These Neolithic people combined hunting with primitive farming. They developed more efficient stone axes and other work tools with which they cleared the native woodland to create open areas on which they grew primitive strains of wheat, barley, oats and beans. Through time, domesticated breeds of sheep, cattle and pigs were introduced, and were then bred as native stock. Farming and domestic technology advanced as Neolithic people began to make pottery and to develop and invent more sophisticated implements.

During this early Neolithic period there were probably only a few hundred settlers in West Cornwall. The population of Britain in 2,500 BC is thought to have been somewhere between 10,000 and 20,000, with the highest concentrations being in the south of England. Farming brought social stability. It created surplus food and encouraged a more settled lifestyle. In turn this led to population growth, more permanent settlements and a demand for cultivable land. As more trees were felled and the land was turned to the growing of cereals and to grazing, the only truly 'natural' landscape that ever existed in West Cornwall, as in other parts of Britain, was lost forever. The much-loved 'timeless' landscapes of West Cornwall that we cherish today – to the very cliff edges even and, in places, halfway down the cliffs – owe much of their present nature to human activity.

Most structures that were built by Early Neolithic people were made of woven branches. In time these decayed leaving nothing for archaeologists to pick over. However, recent field work on the Land's End Peninsula has uncovered the stone foundations of a possible Neolithic 'camp' on the granite-studded hilltop of Carn Galver near Gurnard's Head. If it is verified as being Neolithic then this mosaic of rough moorstone, which now lies beneath tangled bracken and gorse, suggests that Neolithic people established more enduring structures on the high ground of the Land's End Peninsula over 4,000 years ago. One hypothesis is that Neolithic sites of this type might have been used as social and cultural gathering points that were visited by a wider community of Neolithic farmers. Another hypothesis suggests that the great headlands of the Land's End Peninsula such as Gurnard's Head, Cape Cornwall and Logan Rock might also have served as Late Neolithic and then Bronze Age gathering points before their use by Iron Age communities.

These Neolithic people were not 'Cornish' in the way that Cornish people of today see themselves as being. They had no self-awareness of being 'British' either; nor did they call themselves 'Celts', the romantic, invented label that our sentimental age attaches to the pre-Roman occupants of Britain. They were certainly 'local', however, and they had begun to shape, without being aware of doing so, the landscape and the Cornish culture that inspires so much enjoyable nostalgia and sentimentality today. Life in Neolithic Cornwall was probably not comfortable in modern terms. It would have been punishing physically. Records have shown that the average height of Neolithic people was a few inches less than the average of today. They were probably dark-skinned and hirsute, an appearance exaggerated by the well-finished animal skins that they wore. They would have been mostly lean and wiry. Obesity was probably unknown. The physically unfit, the disabled, the seriously ill and those newborn who were seriously deformed might not have been allowed to survive.

It was rare for people to live beyond the age of fifty; a forty-year old would be elderly in the modern sense. Women might have lived into their twenties, men into their thirties. Skeletal remains of the period, found as far apart as Orkney and Syria, indicate that Neolithic farming people had healthy teeth that were, however, badly worn from chewing grain that had been only roughly ground. There is no record of

"...the great headlands of the Land's End Peninsula might also have served as Late Neolithic and then Bronze Age gathering points"

Opposite page
"... the wind-sculpted forms
of the ancient rocks..."
Ander Gunn.

Above
Zennor Quoit.
Simon Cook.

the diseases and illnesses suffered by Neolithic people, though they would have had the minor upsets and wounds that we suffer from. Skeletons show, however, that many adults had arthritis and other bone diseases that had not been evident amongst their hunter-gatherer predecessors, whose main activity was hunting animals on foot. The women of the Neolithic farming communities suffered from crushed vertebrae and damaged knee-joints, possibly because of long periods spent on their knees grinding corn by hand. Bad backs and ruined joints were common because of damage caused by heavy lifting and pulling. Such problems are evident still among men and women in West Cornwall who have worked in farming, mining and fishing, activities that place damaging stress on the body.

Neolithic people probably had a vocabulary of simple words and sounds; but it is unlikely that there was a Neolithic cultural equivalent of our own 'chattering class'. People would have communicated with each other for mainly practical reasons; for identifying animals and objects, in indicating direction and in organising shared activity such as hunting. Simple gestures might have played an important part in communication and there was probably silent co-ordination between people who were engaged in hunting. Such devices are still in use among people who work closely together, in the open air especially.

Neolithic people had a cultural and spiritual life nonetheless. They measured out their lives and deaths with monuments of stone that seemed to replicate the wind-sculpted forms of the ancient rocks that surrounded them. Their era lasted almost 2,000 years, the same period as the Christian era so far and in that time they developed some forms of spirituality and of expression. At first, it seems that they abandoned their dead to the elements and to scavenging birds and animals, a practice still common among unmodernised societies today. Later generations cremated their dead and placed the remains in containers beneath low mounds of earth. As their society became more hierarchical and began to transform itself into the 'Bronze Age' during the period 2500-1500BC, the corpses of notable people were placed within stylised burial chambers that were constructed on prominent hilltops.

West Cornwall's famous 'quoits', the granite pillars and huge capping stones of chamber tombs that crown the moorland heights of Zennor Hill, Mulfra, Lanyon and Chun are the most substantial artifacts of ancient Cornwall to survive. On the lower ground of the peninsula many more of these tombs must have collapsed and become degraded through time, or were dismantled in land clearances of later centuries. Their massive stones were ideal for recycling in buildings, walls and gateposts by local communities for whom convenience was the priority.

The famous Mên-an-Tol holed stone that stands on the moors between Madron and Morvah was probably the entrance to a chamber tomb that in recent centuries was demolished and then pillaged for its stone. It is one of the most visited sites in West Cornwall and is promoted enthusiastically as an ancient monument. Yet the present holed stone and its flanking pillars were moved and re-erected as late as the 19th century. Their present alignment has no prehistoric significance. The impressive Lanyon Quoit lies a short distance away alongside a public road and is even more accessible. It too was rebuilt after it had collapsed in 1815.

These chamber tombs of the Late Neolithic-Early Bronze Age are called portal dolmens, the latter being a word that derives from the Cornish-Breton word for 'cave of stone'. The word cromlech, from the Welsh for 'crooked' or 'concave' stone, is also used to describe them. The modern term 'quoit' derives from the flat capping stone of these remarkable structures. We are casual with our labels. It would be fascinating to know what names, if any, were given to these ancient monuments by those who built them and then treated them with great reverence.

Erecting monuments of stone required new skills from

Below
Mulfra Quoit, Newmill.
Des Hannigan.

Opposite page
Mên-an-Tol, Bosullow.
Simon Cook.

people whose predecessors had been woodcutters. One theory is that the chambers were constructed by first using leverage and simple pulleys to raise the upright stones. Sloping banks of earth and rubble were piled against these uprights. The vast capping stone was then pulled up the slope and into position by teams of people hauling on thick ropes of plaited hemp that again passed through pulleys. The whole structure was covered finally with a mound of earth, although this last assumption is now questioned by archaeologists. Earth might have been banked up to half-height, but the capping stone and entrance passageway were possibly left exposed.

During the Middle Bronze Age a different type of tomb known as an entrance grave, or chambered cairn, evolved. These were more sophisticated in their structure than the chamber tombs. They comprised passage entranceways that led to chambers and smaller side chambers. The structure was covered in mounds of earth and stones, but the entrance to the passage was left exposed. There are several ruins of entrance graves on the Land's End peninsula, two accessible ones being on roadside sites at Bollowall (Carn Gloose) near St Just and Tregiffian near the

Merry Maidens stone circle. The Bollowall grave is in superb condition, because it was preserved for many years beneath mining rubble. Primitive politics as well as ritual was associated with the building of the chamber tombs and entrance graves. The prominence of the sites and their visibility probably indicated a secondary use as symbolic identifiers; not only the revered tombs of ancestors but also the territorial markers of a society that had become rooted in the landscape.

From about 3,000 BC onwards, Neolithic people began to erect circles of stone pillars. Hundreds of these circles were established throughout Britain and Ireland, but only a few survive in what are now moorland and mountain areas. Very large single standing stones were often erected close to stone circles and seem to have been associated with them. Individual stones called menhirs, from the Breton word for 'long stone', were also erected in isolation.

In West Cornwall many stone circles and standing stones have survived. The best known and most accessible stone circle on the Land's End Peninsula is in a roadside field at Rosemodress just west of

Lamorna. Nineteen stones make up a circle whose present symmetry is probably due to re-alignment in recent centuries. The circle is known as Boleigh or Dawns Maen, 'the stone dance', but its popular name is Merry Maidens, a romantic label derived possibly during the early Christian era from a myth that claimed that several young girls were turned to stone for dancing on the Sabbath. It suited Christian interests to dismiss pagan sites and pagan rituals as primitive 'fairy tales'. Two very tall stone pillars known as The Pipers, located near Boleigh, represent Sabbath-breaking musicians. We relish such fanciful myths today but they have no relevance to the Neolithic circle builders who had no concept of 'maidens', merry or otherwise.

There is no recorded information from the prehistoric era and precious little from the late Iron Age. All we have are the vestigial ancient monuments from which to surmise. The purpose of circles and standing stones can only be guessed at but ceremonial and sacred significance seems likely. The circles might even have been community meeting places where trading was carried out and where social activity took place. Mystery clings to the circles like Cornish mist. They have attracted numerous devotees and theorists who study sun, moon and star alignments of the stones, measure earth forces and indulge in often self-justifying spirituality. Tall stones are matched by tall stories. The dancing of Merry Maidens, the force fields, the ley lines, the customised paganism, the midsummer frolics, the stone-hugging, the compulsion that now draws many people to these calm relics of the 'unwritten years', owe much to modern sentimentality and indulgence. There is no contemporary record, no primary evidence to explain these compelling monuments. This may frustrate our modern desire to analyse everything, to claim empathy with a piece of solid rock and to assume understanding and allegiance with an ancient people. Yet we are eternally fascinated by these ancient artefacts precisely because we cannot explain them fully.

Above
Nine Maidens stone circle, Boskednan, near Madron.
Simon Cook.

Opposite page
Boleigh (Merry Maidens) Circle, Rosemodress, near Lamorna.
Charles Mason-Smith.

The stone circles and standing stones of the Neolithic period are in many ways the last unexplained 'mysteries' of prehistory. By 3,000 BC, however, Late Neolithic people were absorbing the ideas and innovations of European metal-users with whom they came in contact. This was the beginning of a transition to what for long has been known as the 'Bronze Age', a sweeping categorisation of over two thousand years of development that had the technology of metal manufacture at its heart. Copper tools and weapons had been manufactured in Eastern Europe from 4,500 BC, and bronze is believed to have first been used in Thailand as early as 6,000 BC. Before the Bronze Age, arsenic, which was naturally present in copper ore, acted as an incidental hardening agent of the finished metal. As pure copper ore became available it was found that hardening of the finished metal could be achieved by mixing copper with tin in a ratio of eight parts to one. The resulting metal was an alloy that was known as bronze. The name is of unknown origin. Britain was peripheral to these early developments of the Bronze Age and although copper was being mined in Ireland by 2,500 BC, surprisingly there is no evidence of mining in West Cornwall during this early Bronze Age period.

Soon after 2,000 BC economic activity developed quickly throughout Britain. It is now thought that this was due to the influence of advanced Bronze Age 'technicians' who have been labeled 'Beaker People' because their culture coincided with the widespread use of a type of tall pot, or beaker that was decorated with cord markings. The original 'Beaker' people might have been miners and metal-smiths who came from the European landmass to look for sources of tin in West Cornwall. They were probably shamanistic figures, looked up to and admired by the agrarian people of West Cornwall, not least because they proved that there was alternative work to farming and that it was possible for individuals to travel and to make more of their lives. The Beaker culture was associated with such diverse activities as mead drinking and archery. The reason for these cultural changes is complex and reflects a long-term development rather than dramatic overnight change.

Although the Bronze Age introduced new types of work, farming remained the main occupation on the Land's End Peninsula. From 1500 BC onwards, farmers cleared more and more ground of sub-surface stones with which they built the characteristic walled boundaries or 'hedges' that are such attractive features of the north coast of the peninsula. The Bronze Age established continuity of settlement. As family groups stabilised, farmsteads developed on existing Neolithic sites, often obliterating older buildings. Such sites were used by successive generations through to the Iron Age and beyond. Many of today's farms in West Cornwall have a tradition of use reaching back to prehistory; their present dwellings rest on the lost foundations of the Bronze Age and the Neolithic period. Bronze Age dwellings were of the characteristic beehive type. Their low circular walls of stone supported a roughly thatched roof; they formed small groups within the cultivated landscape. By 1500 BC the Land's End Peninsula had a native population that was busily parceling up the land wherever it was usable.

Bronze Age people cremated their dead. They placed the ashes in urns and these, along with personal items, were enclosed in small stone cists. Status had become important even in death. Evidence from surviving sites suggests that quite complex burial

rituals may have taken place in honour of leaders of the community. The cists were covered with mounds of earth that we know as *tumuli*, from the Latin word for swelling. Most people would have been buried in less durable receptacles, though still with respect and some ceremony. In West Cornwall, there were probably hundreds of these cists scattered across the landscape and subsequently lost because of ploughing and field clearance. Bronze Age people also established larger burial sites known as barrows in which it is likely that tribal leaders were buried.

Extraction of tin and copper ore probably began in West Cornwall during the later Bronze Age. Early extraction was from the washed-down deposits of the valleys, but no traces of prehistoric workings have been found. Speculation that West Cornwall was a prehistoric tin-exporting centre has led to St Michael's Mount being claimed as the fabled tin-trading island

of 'Ictis' to which Phoenician traders from Lebanon are said to have made regular visits to collect Cornish tin. The references are anecdotal, however, and are based on the often fanciful reportage of Roman historians.

Cornish tin and copper may have been significant only to a British and North European bronze industry. Phoenician traders had more accessible sources of tin ore within the Mediterranean area, although it is still possible that Cornish minerals may have been exported by boat to France and thence by long-established overland routes to the Mediterranean and on to other countries, including Lebanon. A simple commercial connection of this kind between distant lands and through intermediaries can encourage later generations to assume more direct contact. A similar myth that Joseph of Arimathea brought the youthful Jesus Christ to

Above
St Michael's Mount.
Philip Trevennen.

Opposite page
Iron Age grave, Ding Dong.
Des Hannigan.

St Michael's Mount and to other parts of the West Country seems even more like the wishful thinking of enthusiastic Christians, although an open mind is the best insurance for the sceptic.

From about 700 BC the period known as the Iron Age developed in Britain because of growing trade contacts with Europe and through the adoption by Bronze Age people of new ideas and technology based on the use of iron. The period introduced a more productive, entrepreneurial trend which soon made a significant mark on the ancient landscape of West Cornwall. Iron Age communities incorporated existing Bronze Age sites into hill top enclosures. These were labeled by later ages as castles or forts; there are examples at Lescudjack on the edge of Penzance, Chun in Morvah, and on Trencrom Hill above Lelant. The great Iron Age 'cliff castles' of Gurnard's Head, Kenidjack, and Logan Rock may also have been constructed on established Neolithic-Bronze Age sites.

It is tempting to assume that these hilltop and promontory sites indicate a society that had become more defensive because of territorialism amongst competing tribal groups. Inter-family and tribal dispute did emerge during the Iron Age, because of territorial pressures and because of population increase; but the great enclosures may have been linked simply to stock farming. Another theory suggests that they may have been used by local communities as ceremonial sites and even as markets and clearing houses for the goods of a progressive agrarian society. On this count, the walls, banks and ditches of hill and promontory enclosures may simply have been cosmetic features aimed at giving coherence to a site, while coincidentally acting as a barrier to wild animals, rather than to wild warriors.

During the last centuries BC, in western Britain there was a distinct change of climate as the Atlantic Ocean began to exert stronger influence on weather patterns. The warmer, drier conditions of previous centuries gave way to wetter, windier conditions and in time the soil of the higher ground became sour and infertile. Peat cover increased, the ground became waterlogged and once viable moorland settlements were abandoned. The wheeled plough was used on the richer earth between the high moorland and the still wooded and marshy lower ground. Farmers cleared more land and worked it more intensively than previously, thus obliterating the evidence of land use during the Neolithic-Bronze Age. On the Land's End Peninsula today evidence of these periods is scarce, except on the high moors and wild coast.

The Iron Age farmer used sand and seaweed to improve the ground on which ancient strains of wheat, rye, oats and beans were grown. Larger areas of rough grazing were enclosed by the great sweeping curve of an outer wall. They are known as pounds and fragments of them now lie on rough ground and at the edges of small stone-hedged fields. Many of the pounds were subdivided eventually into fields. There are striking examples of surviving pound walls on the Land's End Peninsula at Amalveor in Towednack parish and at Bodrifty near Newmill.

Inside their hilltop enclosures and in the centre of the land that they farmed the people of the Early Iron Age built settlements of simple round houses. Each house had a low encircling wall crowned by a conical roof of reeds or other natural material. By the Romano-British period many of these settlements had evolved into clusters of more sophisticated 'courtyard' houses. The courtyard house had a central space with rooms leading off. Some had corbelled stone roofs, though rough forms of thatch were still used late into the period. These courtyard settlements seem to be unique to West Cornwall; to date, evidence of similar buildings has not been found anywhere else in Britain.

The sites of the Iron Age villages were well drained and well planned. Preserved and partly re-created examples of the Romano-British period can be seen at Chysauster near Gulval and at Carn Euny near Sancreed. There was variety in village planning. Chysauster has a main street as its focus, while Carn Euny is a random grouping of individual houses. Today, despite some artificiality in the re-modeling of features and in landscaping, these sites are

fascinating, not least for the context they give to their surroundings. On Early Iron Age sites such as Bodrifty near Madron the rougher yet somehow more authentic ruins of villages lie rooted in remote moorland. Associated with Iron Age villages are underground chambers known as 'fogous', a word derived from the Cornish for cave. What these intriguing features were used for is not certain but enthusiasts argue passionately over competing claims that they were used as food store, hiding place or ceremonial site. There is a recreated fogou at Carn Euny. The large circular enclosures of the Early Iron Age were still in use in Roman times. Good examples of the type on the Land's End Peninsula are Lesingey Round outside Penzance and Caer Bran in Sancreed. Many other sites are likely to have been destroyed. A round was a single ditch-and-bank enclosure with a cluster of circular houses sited against a section of inner wall. Some archaeologists suggest that these enclosed camps were the homes of influential local leaders.

There was little change in the pattern of Iron Age settlement in West Cornwall during the Roman period. Exeter was the focus of Roman civic power in South West England. The most westerly Roman fort was on the River Camel and Cornwall saw none of the sustained militarisation that occurred in Wales and Scotland. The Iron Age Britons of West Cornwall sought co-operation rather than conflict, being cannier than the Welsh and Scots, perhaps. The Roman writer Diodorus Siculus said of them; *"The natives of that part of Britain, which is called Belerium, are not only very hospitable, but also are civilised in their living, through the intercourse which they have kept up with the merchants of foreign countries,"* a probable reference to tin trading connections between Cornwall and mainland Europe. Roman coins and pottery have been found on numerous sites on the Land's End Peninsula. The Romans took much of their tin from Spain, but it is possible that they traded for some Cornish ore from the tin streamers of the valleys and the surface miners of the moors.

The period between the fifth and tenth centuries is stuck with the label 'Dark Ages', a misnomer from which the period is wrongly assumed to have been anarchic. The Dark Ages were not so much 'dark' with

Top
Early Iron Age stone hut, Bodrifty, Newmill.
Des Hannigan.

Right
Lanyon Quoit.
Ian Kingsnorth.

trouble and strife as simply difficult to analyse, because of a lack of historical record. These were rough times, of course, not least because of the devastating collapse of the British economy after Roman withdrawal. Life on the Land's End Peninsula was more likely to have continued in its complex, but still fruitful way, not least because of those strong economic ties of seaborne trade with Europe. For many centuries, life in a larger Britain barely touched the far west of Cornwall. Even the so-called Saxon 'invasion' of Britain was initially more by default than by aggressive domination and Saxon influence did not extend to the far west of Cornwall until the reign of Athelstan in the early 10th century.

It was during the Dark Ages that the 'native' people of West Cornwall began to emerge as an identifiable ethnic group. Upon this Romano-British-Cornish world descended the famous 'Saints' of Christianised Ireland and Wales. They influenced the economic life of the native Cornish in the same way that the Beaker People did during the Neolithic-Bronze Age. The much vaunted 'saintliness' of these colonisers was underpinned by commercial interest. Myth has obscured how much the civilizing influence of the Irish and Welsh Saints was that of the merchant and peddler of goods as well as of religious and cultural ideas. The Saints brought to the region another important injection of the ancient culture that has been romantically labeled as 'Celtic' and that still distinguishes West Cornwall today.

Coincident with this saintly influence was a rapid advance of agriculture that saw the wholesale clearance of the wooded lower ground of the Land's End Peninsula. As the population expanded, more

ground was cleared. '*All gird themselves to work, they cut down trees, root up bushes, tear up brambles and tangled thorns, and soon convert a dense wood into an open clearing,*' was how a contemporary writer described the clearance work of those early centuries. The language of the early Cornish developed through time. Much of this development was due to the influence of the more sophisticated language forms of the Irish 'Saints' on an earlier Iron Age tongue that had sparse echoes of Neolithic and Bronze Age speech and a sprinkling of Dog Latin embedded within it. The Cornish language that emerged sustained a Cornish identity for centuries; but it was a language that became all too vulnerable to erosion by English influence until it became a spoken form only and then became defunct. Today, enthusiasts for the language struggle passionately to revive the ancient resonance that echoes still in the rich cadences and inflexions of the West Cornwall dialect, as melodic as the sound of the sea and of the moorland wind.

Within West Cornwall especially, thousands of 'Celtic' place names have survived, often corrupted but authentic still. Place names are the most powerful emblems of a region's identity. It is not so much blood ties that confirm Cornish identity; it is the awareness and pride of place that harks back across generations through the language of the landscape.

It was a powerful Cornish identity, underpinned by a distinctive Cornish language, that resisted the Anglo Saxon and later Norman influences of subsequent centuries. The Cornish in the far west resisted Anglicisation, not with arms or empty pride but by rootedness and self-awareness. They continued to farm their land with careful attention to new ideas but with Cornish judgement. They carried on trade and cultural exchange with France. They adjusted English governance to their own ways and were helped in doing so by an earlier Anglo Saxon acceptance of Cornwall as a 'separate' and special place. The Anglo Saxons had assimilated Cornwall politically as a Duchy and thus left its regional identity intact. In turn the Cornish absorbed some of the culture of the larger nation. It is this uniqueness that distinguishes West Cornwall and its people today and that has been shaped and sustained even more by the spectacular landscape of the Land's End Peninsula.

Top
A 'Celtic' Cross: legacy of the Cornish 'Saints'.
Simon Cook.

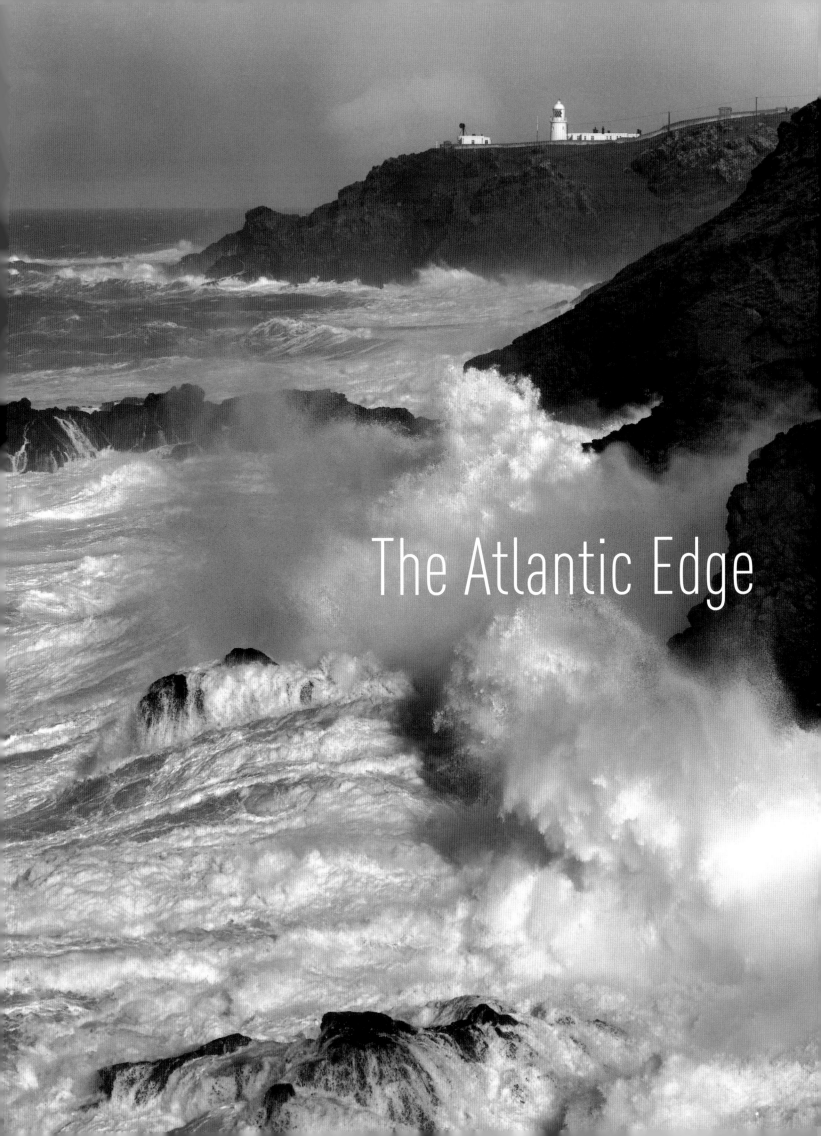

The Atlantic Edge

The Atlantic Edge

The immensity of the 'blue boundless sea' makes the West Cornwall coastline exhilarating. All the great headlands are framed by the sea; the eye is drawn always to the Atlantic – next stop, America. Nowhere else in Britain does the sea dominate with such presence.

The coast of the Land's End Peninsula is a diverse landscape of sheer cliffs interspersed with steep, vegetated slopes. This great curtain wall of rock and earth is breached by a few sandy bays and by narrow valleys that reach the sea at rocky openings known as coves. Bold headlands add to the diversity. Along the clifftops the Countryside Commission's Cornwall Coast Path is drawn like a neat parting through the heathy ground. Further inland, public roads follow a scenic route that merges coast with countryside.

St Ives Bay is a good starting point from which to begin an exploration of this breathtaking coastline. From the northern edge of the bay, at Godrevy Point, the bay shore runs in an arc of golden sand, the Hayle Towans, to its midway point at the mouth of the Hayle River and on to St Ives. The lighthouse on Godrevy Island is ringed with a lime-washed wall that seen from the high mainland cliff looks like a neat white collar drawn round the neck of the lighthouse. From the island a ragged, undersea reef runs for a mile into the sea to where a lonely buoy marks the breaking ledges of Tide Rock and The Heva. The land gives way with reluctance on this Atlantic Edge.

The dunes of Hayle Towans are locked in place by marram grass and white-flowered bindweed. The sea uncurls on acres of clean sand below the dunes and rolls deeply at the northern end of the beach onto a surfers' shore. In summer, these dunes are starred with lilac sea thistle and yellow groundsel. On fresh, blue-skied days a sea breeze whispers through the blades of marram grass; the sand is silver-white; the sea glitters with a diamond light.

Where the Towans end bluntly at Hayle River, the channel that leads from seaward into the river's mouth is marked along its western edge by tall wooden poles on which cormorants perch with wings outspread. For years the channel has given seaborne entrance to Hayle, a town with great maritime and industrial traditions. Once, tall ships berthed two miles inland from these channel markers. During the 19th century and into the early 20th century, Hayle was the workshop of the Cornish mining industry and supplied engines and equipment to mines abroad.

West of the channel entrance the light gleams on wave-rippled sand that seems to run for ever towards distant lines of surf at low tide. Above the beach the low, vegetated cliffs of Carbis Bay make a vivid contrast to this sandy sea-washed environment. The dense green of the wooded cliffs is matched by the green of the swelling water round the massive wall of St Ives harbour where a dark skirt of seaweed trails from the high tide mark.

St Ives is knee-deep in the sea. Tourism has in some ways overpowered this seagoing town whose generations of fishing families looked outwards to the ocean. During the 19th century St Ives developed a residential hinterland linked to trade and mining. But the heart of the town is still its harbour area, the famous 'Downlong', where functional granite buildings merge with the rocky shoreline and the always changing face of the sea. Downlong's vernacular architecture springs naturally from its surroundings and is now the enduring attraction of St Ives for visitors and for the artists who have enhanced and promoted its image.

St Ives has always been a vivid, visual place, not least because of the naturalistic forms of its buildings, the

dramatic beauty of its sea-dominated world and its image-rich harbour life; the whole is given added lustre by the clear and brilliant light of West Cornwall. The influential artists J M Whistler and Walter Sickert visited St Ives in the 1880s and were soon followed by others, many of whom were involved with a more cohesive group of painters, known as the Newlyn School, on the other side of the peninsula. This early connection between St Ives and the world of Art progressed not least through the inspirational work of the self-taught local painter Alfred Wallis and his seminal influence on the young painters Ben Nicholson and Christopher Wood, who 'discovered' Wallis on their first visit to St Ives in 1928. Of the two, Nicholson and his second wife, the sculptor Barbara Hepworth, became hugely influential in the evolution of St Ives within the international Art world. After the

war of 1939-45, younger artists from within Cornwall as well as from outside were drawn to St Ives. The progressive, abstract work of such outstanding painters as Peter Lanyon, Patrick Heron and Sir Terry Frost led to the emergence of the modernist St Ives' School and ultimately to the town's role as a major centre of the Arts.

St Ives may be the preserve of the artists whose century and more of occupation is now celebrated by the bone-white splendour of the St Ives Tate Gallery, but the essence of the town is still glimpsed in the faces of those local people who are, emphatically, a part of the harbour scene. The true face of St Ives is best viewed from the sea.

From St Ives to Zennor Head, the coastline weaves in

Above
St Ives Harbour.
Simon Cook.

Opposite page – left
Cornish stone hedge,
Coronation House,
Bosullow.
Des Hannigan.

Opposite page – right
Iron Age field systems,
Rosemergy, Morvah.
Des Hannigan.

and out of those narrow rocky chasms called zawns, once described tellingly as 'yawns in a cliff'. The rock here is not the ubiquitous golden granite of the promotional brochure. This is the more ancient country rock that the molten granite transformed into dark multi-hued sheets of hornfels and greenstone. Only at Wicca Pool, a mile northeast of Zennor Head is the underlying granite exposed along this section of the north coast. At the tide-line the black rocks are sleek as sealskin where they protrude from swirling Sargassos of thongweed and bladderwrack. The gloomy cliffs are patched with dripping sedge, bright green against the dark rock; on the barest cliffs, paint-like smears of birdlime drain from the nesting ledges of shags and fulmars. Rock samphire and straggling sea beet are rooted in cracks and pockets.

The isolation of this coast is remarkable compared with the bustle of St Ives. The ground on top of the cliffs can be very wet and boggy. The landscape is sombre and desolate in winter; but in summer brightly coloured damselflies and dragonflies flicker amidst the purple moor grass and black bog rush. Where the ground is drier a maritime heath of bell heather, ling and western gorse is speckled with yellow tormentil and purple orchid. Dense patches of bramble and bracken swamp the sheltered hollows. For half a mile inland Lilliputian fields are stitched together by overgrown stone hedges that originated as piles of stone cleared from the ground by Bronze Age and Iron Age farmers.

Throughout West Cornwall the style of these hedges varies greatly. Hedges on rough moorland and scrubland consist of layers of stones piled on top of massive boulders called grounders. Hedges in more ordered countryside, and alongside roads and lanes, are often broad and high. They are built of a framework of stones infilled with earth, and with earth packed between the individual stones. Vegetation roots deeply into the mass and binds the wall together with a deluge of grass, moss and brightly coloured wild flowers.

On the north coast, the unseen boundary between country rock and granite lies two hundred yards inland from the cliffs. The contrast between the rock types is emphasised by the black, sea-stained coastal cliffs and the silver-grey granite tors that lie bedded amidst yellow gorse and plumed bracken on Rosewall Hill and Zennor Hill. The stone-peppered Zennor Hill was a natural quarry for centuries; Zennor moorstone was used to build the handsome tower of St Ives church and today, half-finished blocks of granite still lie marooned where the old stonemasons abandoned them amidst the windblown grass of the hills.
The line of cliffs is broken three miles west of St Ives where the Treveal stream flows through a wooded valley. In summer the banks of the stream are dense with willow and elder and tall blackthorn. Royal Fern and creamy-headed umbellifers thrive in this wetland where goldcrests, linnets and spotted flycatchers breed and where red admiral and painted lady butterflies perch on the glistening leaves.
From Treveal, the coast traces a chaotic line towards Zennor Head from where sheer cliffs plunge for two hundred feet into the sea. The cliffs are bearded with lime-coloured *sea ivory* lichen on the upper walls. On the lower walls, in the bronze light of summer sunsets, *xanthoria* lichen adds brilliant blotches of yellow to the dark rock.

The steep-sided bay west of Zennor Head is Pendower Cove. The sea here can be as smooth as silk in quiet

weather. Pendower is enshrined in folklore as the place from where a fanciful mermaid drew down a young local man whose sweet singing voice enchanted her. Such myths endure; at first because of fond sentimentality and then because they become pinned like a tiresome label on the image of a place. The Mermaid of Zennor is worth a passing glance. Zennor, within its exquisite landscape, is far more absorbing.

Iron Age field patterns are clearly seen in the parish of Zennor in the form of webs of stone-hedged enclosures spreading out from central farmsteads. The pattern has been absorbed into the overall scheme that sets each coastal farm within a broad corridor of land that leads from rough grazing at the cliff edge, through cultivated fields and then to more rough grazing on the moorland hills. Creating these patchworked fields is how men and woman first

measured out survival in this grudging landscape, long before we grew to admire and cherish it for its beauty alone.

There are other striking reminders of the Iron Age. A mile west of Zennor, the great promontory of Gurnard's Head juts into the sea; its name reflects the knuckly, fish head profile of its outer point. Its older name of Trereen Dinas, 'castle on the hill', reflects its Iron Age status as a fortified enclosure. Low cliffs fringe the eastern side of Gurnard's Head where the vestigial remains of Iron Age houses are visible on the grassy slopes above. Rocky ramparts still span the neck of the promontory but are not easily identified today. Occupation of the site may have been seasonal. Fragments of Iron Age Breton pottery found here supports the view that the settlement was a trading centre, an indication of early links between West Cornwall and Brittany.

Above
The shining sea.
Bob Berry.

Opposite page – top
'...its colours are bronze...'
Bob Berry.

Opposite page – bottom
Quiet seas at Carn Gloose,
with Gurnard's Head
beyond.
Des Hannigan.

Fearsome black walls plunge two hundred feet into the sea on the south side of Gurnard's Head. Beyond here, dark, menacing cliffs wind in and out of echoing zawns through the craggy wilderness of Pedn Kei and the hidden and spectacular Zawn Duel. The zawn is three hundred feet deep; the deepest in all of West Cornwall. Above the cliffs, in summer, the grassy slopes are bright with pink-headed thrift and creamy sea campion; the air is sweet with the aromatic smell of sea carrot.

Beyond Zawn Duel and the huge undercut cliff of Carn Gloose, the dark hornfels and greenstones run out at Porthmeor Cove. Here, a shallow valley leads inland along the dividing line of metamorphic rock and granite. The rock-studded slopes of Carn Galver rise steeply from the coast road to a ragged tor-crowned ridge from where the moorland hills crowd towards the sea once more, the granite spilling down to the great golden cliff at Bosigran above a shining sea. The granite is monumental in scale; its colours are bronze and ochre. In the golden light of the sun it sparkles with quartz and felspar; in dull weather it is silver-grey; a chameleon rock that enhances the variegated greens and browns of the cliff slopes.

At Bosigran, Zennor gives way to the granite parish of Morvah, that 'most cold seat in winter' according to the Elizabethan writer John Norden, who must have had a tender nose for hard winds from the sea. Morvah is the archetypal West Cornwall parish. It comprises a tiny hamlet, a sturdy granite church, farmsteads and clusters of houses amidst a few square miles of tawny moorland and stone-hedged fields. Morvah's fields run to the edge of vast echoing cliffs where waterfalls plunge through the air as curtains of spray, or are blown back from the cliff

edge by the tearing onshore winds that can send balls of sea foam whirling a mile inland.

From this now sparsely populated parish, during the 18th and 19th centuries, scores of miners once took their energy and spirit below ground to work the local mines of Carn Galver, Garden Mine and Morvah Consols. When the work failed them they took that energy and spirit to distant lands. Today the bare roots of their cottage walls lie engulfed in grass and bracken. Below ground, in barely accessible caverns and adit tunnels, broken rails and sagging timbers slowly decay. On rock ledges, huge iron buckets, known as kibbles, stand intact. They are so oxidised that a mere touch will reduce sections of them to powder. It is said that rich lodes of copper still lie beneath the Morvah coast.

The Morvah mines were peripheral mines however. The heartland of Cornish mining lies to the west of Morvah where the granite dips beneath the dark metamorphic rock once more and where the faultlines between granite and country rock bloomed with mineral lodes. Beyond the black cliffs and the squat rounded tower of the lighthouse at Pendeen Watch lies the true mining coast of West Cornwall, the clifflands of Trewellard, Botallack, Kenidjack and Cape Cornwall.
This is a hard and desolate landscape; more so since the last working mine in the area, at Geevor, finally ceased production in 1990. The cliffs here are less picturesque than the granite cliffs of Morvah, though they are no less dramatic. Their hinterland is industrial. Two centuries of heavy mining have left a

Heritage Site that celebrates the relics of Victorian tin and copper mining at various sites on Dartmoor, in Central Cornwall and at most of Cornwall's coastal mining areas.

A strong focus of the mining heritage of the Pendeen and St Just area is the excellent Geevor Tin Mine museum with site tours, exhibitions and interpretive material that outline the story of Cornish coastal mining and give a strong impression of a punishing but ennobling trade. The human face to all of this is found in the adjoining settlements of Bojewyan, Boscaswell, Pendeen, Trewellard and Carnyorth, where the linear pattern of small granite cottages reflects the interdependence of mines and people. The mines may have closed, but in these resilient communities a powerful self-awareness and sense of place survives.

ragged palimpsest of decay and chaos that has yet acquired a rough beauty, not least because of the sea's dramatic presence. This was an industry that made no concessions to the environment. While the last of the mines was operating, muddy waste water from the processing works drained into a sea that was stained blood-red with iron oxide for hundreds of yards along the shoreline. It bred good lobsters, they say. When storms whipped the sea into turmoil the clefts in the dark cliffs at Pendeen overflowed with surreal billows of pink foam.

Today this mining coast is a major part of a World

Beneath the ground and beneath the sea, mile upon mile of mine workings slice through the rock. The network of shafts, levels inclines and adits is of such complexity and age that it's full extent is not known. Shafts descend for hundreds of metres; levels and inclines run for over a mile beneath the seabed. But there is no lively echo of the past in these deep mines, only a muffled silence in the few levels that

"Beneath the ground and beneath the sea, mile upon mile of workings slice through the rock"

remain unflooded by the water that has drowned, probably for ever, the aspirations of the hard rock coastal miner.

Above ground the relics of mineral mining lie embedded in the landscape. Along the coast from Geevor stands the National Trust's Levant engine house, where the silken power of steam is enshrined in the form of a working beam engine that is 'fired up' on certain days. Farther west at Botallack, the preserved engine houses of the famous Crowns Mine stand on spectacular rocky promontories, their granite walls seeming to grow naturally from the jet-black killas cliffs that plunge beneath. From these buildings an incline, down which wagons ran, led into a tunnel mouth that gave access to miles of undersea workings. Today, the gantries, tracks and cables of the incline are long gone, as are all the perishable artifacts that mantled this one-time industrial

landscape, a landscape that has now recaptured much of its natural beauty. The surviving engine houses and chimneystacks, with their elegant rustic architecture and their granite walls, enhance that beauty today.

Hidden within the landscape are the most dramatic mining remains of all. These include the remains of ancient tunnels known as 'bunnys' or 'tin floors', large deposits of tin ore that were laid down horizontally, compared to the more common vertical lodes. These bunnys were the first large excavations to be made by medieval or earlier tinners who exploited the seams of rich ore from the surface.

Amidst the glistening rocks at sea level, old chains and bolts are welded by rust to the base of tidal pools; they look like the bones of rusty skeletons. In the cliff faces, gloomy openings lead to where shafts drop into the watery darkness. Everywhere there is evidence of excavated platforms and tracks, the foundations of a vast network of trestles, chains, cables, tramways, launders and walkways that filled the gaunt spaces between the surviving buildings.

Beyond Botallack, the decaying mine stacks post the way towards Kenidjack Head and into the deep trough of Nancherrow Valley, scene of intensive mining during the 18th and 19th centuries. The seaward end of the valley is dominated by a huge wheel-pit that served the Wheal Call mine. The massive stonework and the style of the building give it the look of a medieval fortress. The giant wheel that once filled the pit was driven by water. On the slopes above are the straight lines of channels, known as leats, that led from storage ponds high in the valley and brought water power to dozens of smaller wheels and crushing stamps.

Nancherrow once bustled with vigorous life, although the landscape was wasted and poisoned beneath the creaking, rattling web of trestles and overhead flat-rods, amidst calciners, arsenic labyrinths, mine stacks, dressing floors, spoil heaps, ponds and water wheels. The air was dense with choking smoke and fumes. Water brought power and sluicing action, but it destroyed also; it drowned men below ground and soon after the last mine closed in 1892, a flash flood from the high moorland poured down the valley with devastating force in a last dismissal of a failing industry.

The Nancherrow Valley opens onto the rocky bay of Porthledden on whose southern edge Cape Cornwall swells voluptuously to its shapely summit. The Cape defines the notional dividing line between the two great seaways of St George's Channel and the English Channel. It was known to medieval sailors as the true 'Land's End' because it was thought of at the time as being the most westerly point on the peninsula. On the southern side of the Cape is Priest's Cove, where fishermen work small boats from a slipway area still scattered reassuringly with the clutter of active seagoing.

"The sea dominates here and the Atlantic breakers ride uninterruptedly onto the shining sand"

Opposite page
*Sennen Cove lifeboat slip
and breakwater.*
Ander Gunn.

Above
*Enys Dodnan and the Armed
Knight; Land's End.*
Simon Cook.

South of the Cape is the high headland of Carn Gloose from where the view south is to Land's End and the Longships Lighthouse. A mile inland from the Cape is the town of St Just, still the resilient heart of the mining district and the commercial centre of this northern part of the Land's End Peninsula. The sturdy granite buildings that surround a spacious market square define St Just. At the eastern side of the square stands the fifteenth century parish church, a handsome Norman building of weathered granite. To the west of the square, at the end of a narrow street, is the stern Victorian facade of the Wesleyan Methodist Church. It is a spacious building, yet it could barely accommodate the hundreds of worshippers who flocked to it during the mining heyday of what was a righteous and strong-willed Cornish town.

South of Carn Gloose the coastline drops steeply into Porthnanven, a boulder-strewn cove at the mouth of the sheltered Cot Valley. There is a spectacular raised beach above the rocky foreshore, its earthy, vertical face peppered with rounded, sea-polished boulders. From Porthnanven a line of low cliffs snakes in and out of small bays where granite boulders, shining white, fill the small beaches. Clutches of gleaming black dolerite boulders are scattered amongst them. Within a mile or two, the great surfing beaches of Whitesand Bay flatten the profile of the coast. The sea dominates here and the Atlantic breakers ride uninterruptedly onto the shining sand and fill the air with the scrubbed, salty smell of the open sea. At the southern edge of Whitesand Bay is the village of Sennen Cove where Cornwall and the Atlantic meet head on beneath vast skies. From this tenuous foothold the RNLI's Sennen lifeboat and its crew maintain the great traditions of skill and service that are the hallmarks of Cornwall's lifeboat men and women.

Beyond Sennen Cove and the bare-knuckled granite cliffs at Pedn-mên-du, the coast runs on to Land's

End, the symbolic focus of the dwindling peninsula, the Belerium of the Romans, the 'Seat of Storms'. To the sailors of old it would have been of little account which of the beetling headlands that ring this spectacular stretch of coast was the symbolic Land's End. Each headland was a desperate hazard to sailing ships caught against a lee shore. Even today a close view of Land's End from seaward puts a sharper edge to the headland's mystique. But for the land-based visitor that mystique is irresistible. Land's End has drawn pilgrims for centuries. In 1698 the great Elizabethan traveller Celia Fiennes visited the barren rocks. Fiennes established a healthy precedent when she wrote, *"I clambr'd over them as farre as safety permitted me."* In modern times, the same compulsion has drawn vast numbers of people to the Land's End complex where tourism has distilled the history, the romantic traditions, myths and legends of

centuries into a persuasive brew. As always, however, Cornwall keeps many of its secrets below ground, unseen and unreachable. In the great cavern that slices through the area's northern promontory of Dr. Syntax's Head, huge granite boulders, like dinosaurs' eggs, nestle eerily in the raised galleries of ancient sea beds.

From Land's End to the south east, the coastline takes on a sunnier aspect than that of the powerful but often gloomy cliffs of the north coast. From this western arm of Mount's Bay the view is to the beautiful south. The flatness of the clifftop lends a greater sense of airy distance, of space and freedom. The fall of golden granite is more precise, more heart-stopping. The cliffs take on their most elegant geometric forms, especially at the promontories of Pordenack, Carn Boel, Carn Les Boel and Gwennap

Above
Logan Rock, Porthcurno Bay.
Simon Cook.

Opposite page
Flying the flag for the fishermen.
Simon Cook.

Head, where wind-eroded slabs and pinnacles soar from the tide-line to grass. Between each stretch of protruding cliff the sea has bitten into the weaker rock to form shallow bays where the granite of the pinnacles is friable and hollow and has the texture and colour of terra cotta.

Above the sea-washed lower walls of the great cliffs, green tongues of vegetation fill the gullies and cloak the ledges with fat cushions of pink thrift and sea campion. The honey-coloured boulders are draped with bearded lichen and pink-white stonecrop. During March and April the slopes above the cliffs are thick with the fleshy-leafed scurvy grass; its white flowers fill the air with a sweetly astringent smell. The sea is confined between the headlands and within narrow zawns. But it runs exuberantly into the great mouth of Mill Bay of Nanjizal, where curved swells, a mile across, uncurl on boulder beach and stretches of shifting sand. Minerals were found along this southern shore, although they were in short supply. Above the low cliffs of Mill Bay, the muddy openings of adits still gape from the hillside.

The great promontory of Carn Les Boel lies between Mill Bay and Pendower Cove. On the precipitous eastern edge of the headland, a narrow channel separates the mainland cliff from the huge pinnacle of Bosistow Island. The air is filled with the echoing call of sea birds and in the vast sea-caves that pierce the tall cliffs, Grey Seals birth their young on the sandy floors. The pups drift in and out of the crystal clear channels; their plaintive calls mingle with the screams of the birds and the song of the sea.

The run of high cliffs culminates at the magnificent Gwennap Head where the flood tide from the south divides and sends one great stream eastwards towards the Dover Straits and another northwards through the Irish Channel. The sea is always uneasy here. In storming westerlies, wings of spray climb halfway up the golden pinnacles and rust-red walls of Chair Ladder Cliff. Gwennap is the most southerly point in West Cornwall. This is the 'Fishermen's Land's End', where the Atlantic swell thuds into the dipping bows of outward bound vessels. It is also known as Tol Pedn, the 'holed headland', so named because at its south-eastern edge a gaping hole pierces the grassy surface of the cliff top. There are several of these features on the Cornish coast. They are created when the eroding force of the sea scoops out a cavern at the base of a cliff. Eventually, the weakened upper plug of earth and rock collapses into the cavern below. A mile offshore from Gwennap Head, the

Runnelstone Buoy rolls on the heaving water at the outer end of an undersea reef. Onshore, the fixed swell of the downs replicates the roll of the ocean. During Autumn, when this southerly landfall draws migrating birds of the rarest kind, the downs are carpeted with purple heather and yellow, almond-scented gorse.

From Gwennap Head, the coast turns sharply to the east, as if to pull back from the raw flow of the westerly sea. At Porthgwarra Cove, just east of the headland, the low friable cliffs are pierced by a tunnel hacked out of the rock and through which farmers once drove their carts to collect from the tiny beach seaweed for use as fertiliser. Small fishing boats are still worked from the steep slipway here, but the hard run of the sea beyond the sheltering headland makes it difficult work.

East of Porthgwarra the cliffs fall off in height, though they are still complex and beautiful. At Porth Chapel a crescent of sand marks the seaward end of a shallow valley that wriggles inland to where the rugged little church of St Selevan stands landlocked behind sheltering banks. To the east of Porth Chapel a tumbled chaos of granite encloses the headland of

Pedn-men-an-mere. The rock-studded cliffscape merges seamlessly with the open-air Minack Theatre, the scene of numerous summer productions that are played out against the biggest natural backdrop in the world. The Minack crowns the western arm of the magnificent Porthcurno Bay, where beaches of golden shell-sand line the base of the cliffs at the edge of a turquoise sea.

Porthcurno Bay is enclosed at its eastern end by the spectacular promontory of Treryn Dinas. This great pinnacled headland was the site of an embanked settlement of the Iron Age, similar to its north coast namesake at Gurnard's Head. Treryn Dinas is also known as Logan Rock after the massive rounded boulder that is poised on top of a cluster of pinnacles at its craggy heart. This was a characteristic 'loggan' stone that was once balanced so delicately that it would vibrate at the push of a finger. A notorious dislodging of the rock by a naval party in 1824 and its subsequent re-installation has left the sixty-ton stone more solidly bedded, though its fame is undiminished. It was a tourist attraction from the earliest years of last century when local guides led visitors to the rock.

"...where beaches of golden shell-sand line the base of the cliffs at the edge of a turquoise sea"

Left
Porth Chapel, St Levan.
Des Hannigan.

Opposite page
Mousehole Harbour.
Philip Trevennen.

Along these southern cliffs, the granite has been shaped into striking features. Each one has its local name and all serve as landmarks for the fishermen of Penberth Cove, which lies to the east in the lee of the cliffs. Generations of fishermen have worked their small open boats from its rugged granite slipway. From the mouth of the cove, Penberth Valley runs deep inland. Its slopes are lined with small meadows that once bloomed with violets and produced early potatoes in abundance. Smallholding and market gardening was a flourishing part of the mixed economy of these coastal communities until late this century.

The western shore of Mount's Bay was always something of a vast garden. From Penberth eastwards, there is barely a part of the cliffland that was not turned over to the tiny meadows known as quillets, in which early flowers and vegetables were grown. Today, the slopes are a dense chaos of deep grass, bracken and bramble. Yet a generation ago, the cliff edges were fenced, sometimes with corrugated iron, or whatever came to hand, and the ground 'tealed' and planted with early flowers and vegetables. Where impenetrable vegetation now covers the slopes, horse and cart once negotiated trackways to and from the meadows.

East of Penberth, the cliffs become satisfyingly remote. Broad fields run inland to the distant road. Access to the cliffs is along the coast path from only a few convenient points. It is a sheltered, favoured countryside, except when a south east gale burns across the land with its salty breath. The granite cliffs are still impressive but are subdued by torrents of grass and wild flowers. At Trevedran Cliff, golden monoliths of rock, like Easter Island heads, stud the green slopes. From below the cliff a great barrier of boulders runs along the shoreline to St Loy's Cove. In the deep valley behind the cove daffodils and bluebells flood the ground beneath the trees with vivid colour. White flowered blackthorn trees, sweet chestnut and oak grow thickly to the shoreline.

This is a peaceful coastline on quiet summer days. Yet, a short distance from the lush beauty of St Loy there is a bleak reminder of the sea's brutal indifference. In a small boulder-strewn cove east of Boscawen Point lies the twisted wreckage of the cargo vessel *Union Star* that was driven ashore with the loss of eight people during a murderous storm in December 1981. The local lifeboat, the *Solomon Browne*, based at Penlee Point between Mousehole and Newlyn, rescued four of the coaster's crew in appalling conditions before being itself overwhelmed. The eight lifeboatmen aboard the *Solomon Browne* were lost also. It was the blackest night in the local community's history. Today, the twisted and rusting fragments of the *Union Star* mesh with the seaweed-blackened rocks of the cove; a bleak memorial to immeasurable courage.

The greenstone cliffs at Tater-du, to the east of Boscawen, are a dark contrast to the preceding miles of sun-baked granite. The cliff is jet-black; its features are more angular and square-faced than granite. Yet, the upper part of the cliff shines with a bright yellow frieze of *xanthoria* lichen that is more golden than granite itself. The elegant lighthouse at Tater Du stands at the base of a long flight of rugged steps. It overlooks two offshore rocks called The Bucks and warns of their presence.

The cliff slopes along this coast are swathed in wild daffodils that run in a golden thread all the way to Lamorna Cove and its valley, where the raw wounds of old granite quarries are softened by deep woodland. Beyond Lamorna, the coastline falls off in height to where a fringe of low cliffs leads towards Mousehole. Blurred outlines of overgrown meadows can be seen clearly on the slopes above the cliffs. The quillets and terraced meadows, with their windbreaks of privet and escallonia, lend a flavour of the

Above
Newlyn Harbour.
Simon Cook.

Opposite page
St Michael's Mount.
Philip Trevennen.

Mediterranean to this sun trap corner of Mount's Bay.

The mellowness of the landscape here is a fitting introduction to the inner sanctum of the bay itself. Mousehole is the outlier, a small fishing village with the same architectural coherence as the older parts of St Ives. Beautiful granite walls frame its small harbour. High on the hill above Mousehole is the village of Paul and its fine church, dedicated to the Breton saint Pol de Leon. Deeper into the bay from Mousehole lies Newlyn, a harbour of refuge and a working fishing port of national importance still, in spite of fishing's decline generally. Newlyn is the robust antithesis of quaintness. Its extensive quays and broad tiers of fishing boats and the rattle and hum of its market complex reflect the modern face of a deeply traditional industry. It is an industry that has modernised successfully, though it is faced always with the tightening nets of transnational controls and competition for reduced fish stocks.

It was at Newlyn during the late 19th century that a particular style, or 'School', of painting evolved and set the foundations of West Cornwall's formidable reputation in the Art world. Gifted English painters who had studied and worked in France discovered in the fishing ports of West Cornwall home-based versions of the Breton villages in which they had found their early inspiration. At Newlyn, Penzance and St Ives they found that the clear, accurate light and the colourful world of Cornish fishing especially, provided them with the subjects and the conditions for a new style of art that involved painting out of doors and that was known, after its French origins, as *en plein air*. From this period came the work of such outstanding painters as Stanhope Forbes, Elizabeth Forbes, Frank Bramley, Walter Langley and Norman Garstin, whose work became known collectively as the 'Newlyn School'. Paintings of the Newlyn School can be seen in Penzance's Penlee House Gallery & Museum.

At Newlyn itself, the Newlyn Gallery (redeveloped during 2006-2007) maintains Newlyn's great artistic traditions with exhibitions that are often ground-breaking and thought-provoking and that reflect the current work of British and international artists. The gallery also exhibits the work of accomplished local artists and has a busy educational programme.

Newlyn is connected to Penzance by a mile-long promenade that makes the best of its exhilarating

frontage onto Mount's Bay and that draws the arc of
the bay through Penzance and on towards the
climactic feature of St Michael's Mount. Penzance is a
refreshingly open-faced town, the 'Holy Headland' of
Penwith's 'Peninsula of Saints'. Spanish raiders
destroyed the medieval pattern of its harbour area
during an attack in 1595 and modern urban
development has taken a further toll. But the lower
town has retained its charm, especially in the narrow
Chapel Street that lies between the upper town and
the harbour. The core of the town is a pleasing mix of
Regency and Georgian buildings and there are
beautiful public gardens.

From Penzance, the inner curve of the bay swings

east to Marazion, the oldest chartered town in
Cornwall. Marazion's melodious name derives from
Marghas Byhgan, the Cornish Thursday market, and
defines the town's origins as the site of important
fairs that ensured its prominence until medieval
times. Offshore from Marazion lies St Michael's
Mount, the crowning glory of the bay. Its elegant
castle walls are like a seamless extension of the
rough granite of its rocky crown. Southeast from
Marazion, the coastline is made up of low-lying cliffs
of friable rock that extend to the knuckly headland of
Cudden Point. St Ives Bay is seven miles due north from
here. The journey along the coast's Atlantic Edge is
nearly eight times that distance.

Top
Gwithian, St Ives Bay.
Rob Jewell.

Bottom
*Porthmeor Beach,
St Ives Bay.*
Ian Kingsnorth.

Heartland

Heartland

The dramatic coastline of the Land's End Peninsula gives West Cornwall its unique identity; but the green heart of the peninsula adds another dimension to this already favoured region. From the sea-washed rocks of Godrevy, the land runs south across flat downland and into a fertile and sheltered countryside of fields and woods that are a mellow contrast to the bare-knuckled coast. Scattered throughout this pastoral landscape are pleasant villages such as Angarrack, St Erth, Connor Downs, Gwinear, Carnhell Green and Leedstown where corners are turned down unhurried lanes and where the sea and its clamour seems a world away.

The River Hayle elbows its way east through the heart of this quiet countryside. From Atlantic Ocean to English Channel it is only six green miles. The neck of land is even narrower between Hayle and Marazion, at the true threshold of the Land's End Peninsula. For centuries the quickest way to cross Hayle Estuary was by ferryboat. Heavier traffic had to detour for a mile inland to cross the River Hayle at St Erth Bridge. The causeway that now carries the busy A30 was opened as a turnpike in 1825. It was like the bridging of a river. Until then, the Land's End Peninsula had been a true *'demi- Island in an Island'*.

The main road from Hayle to Penzance follows the edge of high ground between broad fields, where early flowers and bulbs, potatoes and broccoli are grown. The road passes through the villages of Canonstown and Crowlas before veering towards Penzance at Long Rock and the shores of Mounts Bay. At Marazion a large swathe of marshland gives some idea of the ancient wetlands that once lay across the narrow isthmus between Marazion and Hayle.

At Trencrom Hill, to the northwest of the Hayle-Penzance road, the granite spine of the peninsula rears up from a deep fringe of woodland. Trencrom is a natural fortress; its ancient name was Trecrobben, the 'curved hill'. On its green summit are the remains of a prehistoric encampment that may have been Neolithic and that was used certainly by later Iron Age people to command the view to all quarters. From Trencrom the granite landscape unfolds across lonely downs to the west. It rises in a smooth groundswell of patchworked fields and then falls gracefully to the south, to where the village of Nancledra lies in a green fold among low hills. From here, narrow streams flow south to Crowlas and Ludgvan their valley banks shrouded with trees that would be hard pushed to survive on the bare north coast.

The land rises to the west of Nancledra. This is a complex landscape that has been exploited in places for quarrying of stone and for extraction of china clay. On the high hill of Castle an Dinas, the land has been prised apart and wrenched of its stone. Yet the area is still rich in ancient remains. Further west, the countryside is thick with *tumuli*, the mounds of small prehistoric burial sites. At its heart is the preserved Iron Age village of Chysauster.

Narrow lanes lead north from Nancledra to the green fold of the Towednack Valley where the little church of St Tewennocus stands four-square amidst the quiet hills. From here the ground rises once more through swelling fields to the rough moorland of Trendrine Hill, Amalveor and Lady Downs where the familiar spider's web pattern of Iron Age fields is again clearly outlined. On the moorland, the slabby pile of Zennor Quoit marks a Neolithic burial ground. The quoit was plundered of its stone last century to build a cattle shelter. Improvisation was the way of the Victorian farmer as much as it was of the Neolithic farmer.

From Zennor Hill the granite spine of the peninsula undulates westwards across the airy moorland to quoit-crowned Mulfra Hill and the knuckly ridge of Carn Galver above Bosigran. These moors offer little to the farmer other than rough grazing for beef cattle and although some sheep are grazed, the ground is deficient in the cobalt that is necessary for successful sheep rearing.

The variety of plant species is not great on these moors, but the area's value as 'wild' land ensures its survival within the small area of the Land's End Peninsula. Loss of even a few acres of this heathland habitat would mean a serious depletion of flora and fauna. The breaking in of the moorland edge for cultivation, a timeless imperative for farmers from Neolithic times onwards, has now been stemmed. For our modern times, the fragile ecology of this ancient ground deserves respect and the minimum of mechanical intrusion, although some management is beneficial. Burning of moorland areas that have become choked with bracken and bramble and scrubby heather has always been carried out at

permitted times of the year. When it is managed properly this burning, known as 'swaling' leads to improvement of the natural heathland habitat. The balance is fragile, however; too much accidental or careless, uncontrolled burning can cause immediate damage to bird life and insect life and can cause long term damage to the habitat generally.

Ling, bell heather and the yellow-flowered western gorse dominate the peaty soil of the moors. The tiny

"In winter the moors are bleached of their colour; the bracken is sombre and dull brown; the moor grass is as white as snow"

white flowers of bedstraw and the blue of milkwort speckle the moor grass, and all round the rocky carns, bluebells nestle amidst bilberry and heather. By late summer, dense bracken swamps the slopes of the hills; but where the heather and gorse is free of bracken the mosaic of autumn colours is dazzling. On the wetter ground the white buds of cotton grass nod in the breeze amidst tussocks of purple moor grass and soft rush. In damp hollows, willow and blackthorn thrive and offer good habitats for meadow pipit, stonechat and whitethroat. This is buzzard country; the great birds drift lazily in the blue, while skylarks fill the summer air with their sweet, promising song.

In winter the moors are bleached of their colour; the bracken is sombre and dull brown; the moor grass is as white as snow. Real snow can blanket the moors in winter during cold spells. It lies in gleaming drifts across the tumbled ground and dusts the ancient stones with glittering ice. In the aftermath of a snowstorm, the rocky carns are like minuscule Himalaya under the icy blue void of the sky. But the snow rarely lasts, except when it is followed by prolonged periods of northerly winds. Frost is rare on the peninsula's coastal fringes although again there can be exceptions.

Winter gales in West Cornwall are bitter and raw. They drive the sleeting rain across the desolate ground where solitary hawthorn trees bend their backs against the punishing blast, their crowns wind-flattened. The Land's End Peninsula is first in line for Atlantic depressions that topple onto the peninsula, their savage winds blowing from south east first and then veering round the clock, south to south west and then west to north west before dwindling, if pressure builds in the depression's wake. Winter gales are more likely to crowd one behind the other when the wind backs from the north west and the peninsula braces for yet another onslaught.

The highest ground of the northern moors, at Watch Croft above Morvah, lets this fierce weather blow at will across its flat undistinguished summit. Watch Croft is a mere 252 metres high, yet it has a commanding presence on its northern side, where it overlooks Morvah and the vast Atlantic. Ancient mineral pits dimple the crown of the hill and the northern slopes are a warren of old workings amidst engulfing bracken and gorse. West from Watch Croft, the hills become less prominent. The broad moorland undulates gently towards Land's End; its northern slopes swoop down to the sturdy stone walls that enclose the fields of the dairy and beef farms of the northern coastal shelf. On Chun Downs above Morvah, a chain of ancient monuments crowns the moorland crest. The dominant feature is the great enclosure of Chun Castle, an Iron Age settlement whose walls were once fifteen feet high. Today, they are low heaps of rubble, their best stone plundered for other uses over the centuries. Below the settlement lies the site of an Iron Age village and a few hundred metres along the crest of the hill to the west is Chun Quoit, the stone core of a Neolithic burial chamber that has its hooded capstone still in place.

The ground to the south west of Chun Quoit descends gently across a broad sweep of sombre moorland known as Woon Gumpus Common, or more simply, The Gump, before it rises again to the gnarled rocky tor of Kenidjack Carn above St Just. The carn crouches monster-backed amidst rough moorland. Its rocks are darkly mottled and are twisted enough to suit this 'Hooting Carn's' reputation for dancing devils, giant wrestlers and general witchiness; a heady brew best left for wild moon-drenched nights and wilder imaginations. The real world of the moor is every bit as interesting, especially when mist shrouds the rocks and fills the air with the smell of the damp, musty earth or when feathery clouds melt and reform across a blue sky above the green slopes.

On the slopes that descend to the south there are numerous prehistoric remains. They complement the chain of stone-ribbed monuments that lead from Zennor Quoit to the stone circle at Boskednan and on to Chun Quoit. Just below Kenidjack a group of holed stones stands amidst the deep heather; gnomic templates for the sculptor. A few hundred yards south of here, on Truthwall Common, stands the Neolithic stone circle of Tregeseal.

South of Tregeseal Circle, the moorland merges with the farmed country round St Just. Here, the dragon's back of granite is absorbed into the gentle swell of land that rises to a final flourish through the rounded summits of Bartinney Downs and Chapel Carn Brea. The summit of Carn Brea has a long history of human use. It has been the site of a Bronze Age burial chamber, a medieval hermitage, a beacon, and during the Second World War, a military emplacement. It is now in the care of the National Trust.

The land sweeps uninterruptedly from Carn Brea to

"Beyond this final swathe of Cornwall, sea and sky merge into exhilarating emptiness"

Land's End and Sennen. Across this wave-cut platform the sea once curled in great waves that were as tumultuous as the waves that break on Sennen Beach today. The fields here have the look of dull English acres compared with the random enclosures of the north coast. They are broad, flat and wind-blasted, the legacy of hedge clearances during the early 1970s. Beyond this final swathe of Cornwall, sea and sky merge into exhilarating emptiness.

The southern half of the Land's End Peninsula is a gentler landscape than that of the north coast. From the high ground of the moors the ground slopes gently southwards to the shores of Mount's Bay, across fields and wooded valleys. It is a dense countryside that runs in and out of green spaces and deeply wooded shade. Narrow lanes seem to wind effortlessly in circles, but they always reach a destination. A chain of attractive villages lies in a wide arc round Penzance and brings cohesion to the

town's rural hinterland. The village of Madron, with its stately church and its old houses of dressed granite, is perched on the high ground above Penzance. Madron is at the heart of traditional estate lands where the countryside still has something of the picturesque about its broad-leaved woods and great banks of rhododendrons. Nestling below Madron is the National Trust's Trengwainton Garden, famous for its displays of magnolias, acacias, camellias and azaleas.

The structure of farms on the south-facing slopes has changed little since medieval times. Field boundaries are more sharply defined than they are on the higher ground of the peninsula. The deep, well-drained soil is well suited to arable farming and along the sloping ground that borders the A30, at Ludgvan and Gulval, early potatoes and spring flowers are grown. During spring the potato fields are covered with polythene sheets to encourage growth and for a time, the

countryside is transformed into a landscape that seems dotted with gleaming artificial lakes.

The main roads between Penzance, St Just and Land's End are the only major intrusions upon this pastoral landscape that spreads for thousands of acres throughout the southern and western half of the Land's End Peninsula. It is an orderly countryside compared with the more complex and difficult ground of the moorland and the north coast. Yet, though modern farming has adapted the landscape to its needs, much survives of the old lanes, hedgerows and belts of woodland that run between the farms and hamlets. Trees, bushes and tangled undergrowth crowd together for mile after irregular mile along these corridors of uncultivated land. This fruitful chaos of thorn trees, elder, sycamore, ash and beech, is woven together by dog rose and bindweed, bramble and clinging bryony. It nurtures a colourful torrent of wild flowers in its dewy understorey, where butterflies find their summer habitat and a teeming insect life thrives in the humid air.

The stone hedges that parcel up the fields, and the

sturdy farm buildings and isolated cottages, are an essential part of the rich fabric of the landscape. The rough granite faces of old farm buildings are mottled

Above
'...a fertile and sheltered countryside...'
Simon Cook.

Left
Thrift; symbol of the Cornish cliffs.
Simon Cook.

Right
'...the rich fabric of the landscape....'
Liam Addison.

"...a colourful
torrent of
wild flowers
in its dewy
understorey,
where
butterflies find
their summer
habitat..."

with lichen and their roofs are patched with random slates and are crusted with repeated cement washing that has anchored them in place through a thousand winter storms. Inside these old buildings there is a smell of mildew and damp old age and where animals are housed the rich odour of honest farming hangs in the air.

The messiness and muck of even the best-kept farm is somehow reassuring, as is the decay of old farm buildings. Such buildings have grown out of their environment, warts and all. Yet, today, entire farm complexes have been 'converted', their middens turned into cropped grass, their rough yards gravelled and their granite walls stripped and scrubbed and sealed off against the damp Atlantic winds and the machine-gun onslaught of driving rain. We disengage from the raw impact of Atlantic weather at our peril and too much suburbanisation of the countryside erodes its integrity and its complex aesthetic. Complexity and diversity underpin the special quality of West Cornwall. The coastal parishes are given powerful character by the drama of the sea. Yet,

inland there is a more measured tone. Sancreed is the only land-locked parish on the Land's End Peninsula. It is a parish of high ground and windy rounded summits, from where the sea is a distant prospect. The settlement names of Sancreed are singular; Grumbla, Brane and Skimmel Bridge. At the heart of Sancreed is the restored Iron Age village of Carn Euny, where the remnants of the small, circular houses survive in context with the gnarled landscape. Beneath the foundations of the houses are the imprints of earlier Bronze Age dwellings. North east of Carn Euny, on the windy high ground, is the great earthwork of Caer Bran, the encampment of the family and followers of a local Iron Age chieftain. It commands the very heart of the peninsula and has sweeping views to Mount's Bay.

Just over a mile south of Sancreed is the stone circle of Boscawen-un, the most atmospheric of all Cornish circles. It has nineteen stones that surround a leaning pillar and its location, deep within tangled thickets, adds to its appeal. A mile south across fertile fields is the village of St Buryan distinguished by its landmark

church tower, the Christian equivalent of the Neolithic stone circle. St Buryan was founded as a collegiate church by the Anglo Saxon king Athelston in 930 AD. Surviving church records tell of lively secular politics that seemed at times to be of greater importance than the spiritual life. Disputes between church officers and local gentry were ferocious and as entertaining as modern political spats. They included unseemly squabbles over tithes, the percentage payments due to the church from landowners and merchants.

St Buryan seems reassuringly landlocked at the still heart of the Land's End Peninsula. Yet, the ninety-foot tower of the church can be seen from far out at sea and was used as a landmark by Mount's Bay fishermen for many years. Business on great waters is never far away, even from inland West Cornwall. The medieval church at St Buryan once collected tithes from the pilchard fishery at nearby Penberth Cove and the parish extends as far as Lamorna. Its western boundary follows the course of the Penberth River where it meets the bounds of St Levan, the little parish that encompasses the golden beaches of Porthcurno and the peninsula's most southerly knuckle of land at Gwennap Head. North of St Levan, the parish of Sennen unrolls across the final plateau of the Land's End to the great cliffs of the Atlantic Edge.

Top
The Church of St Selevan,
the parish of St Levan.
Des Hannigan.

Left
'rough yards...and granite
walls', Old Carnyorth.
Ander Gunn.

The Living Landscape

The Living Landscape

"...landscape is a passive creature..."
T. S. Eliot. *After Strange Gods,* 1934.

Landscape seems entirely passive without people. The landscape of West Cornwall is admired because of its essentially vacant beauty, its exhilarating emptiness. Such a beautiful landscape is admired also because it is seen as being changeless. It would be foolish to expect, however, that those who live amidst beautiful landscapes should not change, or that they should never change those landscapes.

A beautiful landscape is unforgiving when times are hard. West Cornwall has bred successful, vigorous communities throughout history; but the hard edge of the Atlantic has also sapped the health and the will of many Cornish men and women. Each generation has lost some of its finest to the sea, and mining and farming have taken their toll. In the past, too many Cornish were forced to leave the Land's End Peninsula, especially during historic slumps in the mining industry. A harsh, unforgiving existence was often the reality of life; even when work was available. When work failed, the alternative was emigration. Last century Cornwall lost thousands of its most vigorous working people to the mining countries of the world.

Mechanisation and regulation have seen large numbers of farming people leave the land or disengage from their rural traditions. The fishing industry has been in decline for many years because of diminishing stocks, overly efficient technology and trans-national politics. Mining on the peninsula has ended. The trades and crafts that supported farming, fishing and mining have become scarcer as the core industries declined. Too many young Cornish people still need to leave the west to find work. Communities often feel alienated because of centralised decision-making and because of the uncertainties of modern economics. Such pressures explain, in part, the mixed feelings that local people might have for the aesthetic value of the world in which they live and work. You cannot eat landscape.

Yet, the identity of the people of West Cornwall has been formed by the raw experience of working with their landscape. The Cornish have always been vigorous and independent. They are pragmatic and unsentimental. In the past they have also been fatalistic, although at times in their history the inequities of mercantilism saw them break bounds. In the mining communities, especially, revolutionary fervour often bubbled to the surface, until the charismatic John Wesley brought the antidote of religion to the tensions of eighteenth century life. Methodism gave to ordinary people a spiritual identity and the promise of redemption after a gruelling life. It imprinted itself on the Cornish world and today in West Cornwall, although church and chapel attendances have declined, a non-conformist instinct has been a powerful defence against the harsh uncertainties of farming, fishing and mining and against too much social and cultural modernisation. To some extent, that same instinct has viewed the landscape as being a work place first and foremost.

Farming has been the most resilient of West Cornwall's traditional industries. It is sustained by the resilience of the land itself and though it is under pressure today the local industry survives; its methods are modern, its values traditional. Yet, the structure of modern farming reveals how much the cultural pattern of West Cornwall rural life has changed. Until mechanisation, farming was labour intensive, and until the middle of the 20th century the tradition of small family farms, and of whole communities being involved with the land, survived. From the 1950s onwards, the pace of change was rapid. Change had little time to filter through the generations so that the retired farming people of today are the last to have continuity of experience with the slow, measured pace of the past. Those who were children during the first decades of the 20th

Previous page
Land, Sea and Sky.
Liam Addison.

Left
Priest's Cove.
Simon Cook.

century experienced a rural world that for centuries had changed little in its aspect or in its culture. They counted out their lives by the day rather than by the minute. They moved through an environment that offered richer stimuli than it does today.

That coherence and continuity of rural life has lingered in West Cornwall for longer than in many other parts of Britain. In the late 1950s there were local farmers who still preferred ploughing with horses rather than with machines. During the 1960s there were still farmers on the north coast of the peninsula who struggled to win a living from twenty or so acres. Seaweed was collected for use as fertiliser on reluctant ground.

It was the last gasp of the kind of smallholding life that flourished at the beginning of the 20th century and that bred such men as James Stevens, a Zennor farmer. James Stevens left a plain man's record of his working life, *A Cornish Farmer's Diary* (P. A. S Pool, 1978), a sporadic, but precise record of day to day events at Zennor, and later at Sancreed, between the years 1877 to 1912. His diary is unadorned, yet graphic. It charts some changes in the wider world certainly, but the simple imperatives of a parochial rural life hardly changed throughout Stevens's

lifetime. Work and social life overlapped and religion had a social relevance, as well as a spiritual one. James Stevens's wife, Honor, was herself a Stevens who had been born at St Ives. They had eight children. Honor Stevens would have worked as intensively as her husband at the business of farming, while raising her large family.

Like hundreds of other West Cornwall farmers of the time, James Stevens grew oats and barley, vegetables and fruit. He reared pigs, cows and sheep, and kept bees and poultry. This rich variety of tasks was spiced with hedge making and mending, the cutting of turf and furze and a host of other chores. Most work was

Top
Collecting seaweed.
Ashley Peters.

Left
Modern farming on the shores of Mount's Bay.
Paul Watts.

Right
Shooting fishing gear from the cove boat Seagoblin.
Liam Addison.

done by hand. His work and social life overlapped. Stevens rarely left his Zennor farm, other than to walk across rough moorland tracks to the markets at St Ives or Penzance. In his absorption with husbandry and the rootedness of his life James Stevens was maintaining a tradition that had its source before the Iron Age.

The rhythm of that tradition was maintained for a generation after James Stevens's time. It faltered during the war of 1914-18 but beat as strongly as ever for another twenty-five years. Once again Zennor parish produced a record of those years in the form of Alison Symons's *Tremedda Days*, (1992) an account of Zennor farming life during the first half of this century. It is a much richer book than Stevens's diary and captures the fascinating minutia of farming within the larger experience of life in a beautiful, ancient landscape.

It is on this north coast of the Land's Peninsula that the spirit of ancient West Cornwall is at its most potent. It is in the air itself and in the rich colours of the land above the glittering sea. But the beauty of

the landscape is deceptive. The ground here has always been hard and unrelenting. Even today you need resilience to work in this overpowering landscape where each sunny summer's day is doubly matched by days of driving mist and rain and raw blustering winds. Not much has changed as far as the elements go. The land resists and the sea is restless still. Today's farmers and field workers are still tied to the demanding routine of dairying and the cycle of seasonal work. There are always cold damp mornings to meet; the raw steamy reek of the milking parlour; the driving rain that turns field and yard into a morass. Some crops, including early flowers such as daffodils, are still harvested by hand, often in brutal weather. It is an experience of the landscape that is very different to the experience of those who simply appreciate that landscape for its passive beauty.

West Cornwall has always produced skilled fishermen. The fisherman's trade is timeless. Wherever people settled along the coastline of the peninsula fish were caught. By medieval times fishing had become industrialised as supplies of salt for curing became more readily available. The great

shoals of pelagic fish that have been associated with the Western Approaches for centuries became the staple for such communities as St Ives, Newlyn and Mousehole and the coves of Penberth and Sennen. Until the late 19th century, St Ives was knee-deep in pilchards. Great shoals of fish thronged the inshore waters of the Land's End Peninsula and, at St Ives especially, they seemed to offer themselves up as a sacrifice. The fish seethed along the shoreline in their millions. They were caught in encircling seine nets, which were drawn in close to the town beaches. The fish were scooped into dipper boats from the glittering pool of the net; the air was full of the raw pungent smell of the sea and of oily fish, the sky was full of screaming gulls.

Ashore, the cobbled streets of the harbour quarter, Downlong, stank of blood and oil and the salt sea. The arms and faces of the people were flecked with slime and pilchard scales; their hands and wrists were raw from the constant nimble work. The cellars and courtyards of the harbour area bustled with the work of salting the fish, pressing them for valued oil, and

packing them into hogsheads for export to satisfy the Lenten diet of Italy and Spain. Commerce united Methodist Cornwall with the Catholic Mediterranean. *'Long life to the Pope, death to our best friends, and may our streets run in blood,'* was how the non-conformist Cornish fishermen toasted the pilchard season. Farmers had an interest in the sea also. They bought pilchards cheaply when the market was glutted and enriched their salt-blasted fields with them. Farmers often owned interests in boats and the wealthiest among the seagoing community often branched out into owning farms and rural property.

Today at St Ives the narrow canyons of the streets and alleyways echo still with the sounds of the sea as much as with the chatter of tourists. On winter nights of storming weather, when the granite cobbles gleam in the lamplight and signboards creak in the blustering wind, the raw salty smell of the sea floods in from the open mouth of the harbour. Modern fishing is carried out in an environment that is still harsh and unforgiving and in which frustration with bureaucracy is more acute than it is on land.

"Great shoals of fish thronged the inshore waters of the Land's End Peninsula and, at St Ives especially, they seemed to offer themselves up as a sacrifice"

Technology has not yet subdued the sea or flattened the crest of the wave; the wind still bloweth where it will; the deck of a fishing boat in a gale of wind still tests the strongest. It is a hard life, ill-served by sentimental notions of the fisherman and his trade. We watch the fishing boats leave harbour, bristling with the emblems of their trade and we warm to the adventure and romance of it all. But most of us know nothing of the often brutal realities of that punishing way of life.

The versatility of Cornish fishermen is astonishing. When pilchard fishing declined during the early decades of last century the fishermen of West Cornwall turned to a mixed trade that included working pots for shellfish such as crab, the dark-blue lobster and the rusty-red crawfish. They long-lined for skate, turbot and ling and they trawled for flatfish and cod. Cornish boats still followed what was left of the pilchard trade. They hunted for herring also and took their boats to Scottish and Irish waters. Small boats still work the Cornish shore today, while Newlyn beam trawlers range far into the Western Approaches and gill-net boats run for hundreds of miles into the Bay of Biscay — all with the beleaguered industry in their wake and uncertainty on the wind.

Like the modern farmer, today's fishermen have the advantage of better-equipped vessels that are crammed with electronic aids; but they still have to meet the sea at close quarters. Those who work gear

Left
Ropes at Newlyn Harbour.
Simon Cook.

Top
*Fishermen preparing the
pots in the Atlantic ocean.*
Rob Jewell/W Harvey & Sons.

Right
*'Small boats still workthe
Cornish shore...'*
Steve Martin.

in the traditional manner and from small boats may have the assistance of hydraulics and electronics, but the work is still punishing; the deck still rolls underfoot; the tide can still snatch at pot or gill net and rough ground still snag them until the winch screeches and the boat heels over alarmingly. On bigger vessels there is still the gruelling routine of long days at sea, when darkness and light are the only distinctions between night and day and when a view of the land can be sweet, but never sentimental. There was no sentimentality from the global tin market when Geevor Mine at Pendeen finally closed in 1990. On that bleak day, the great tradition of West Cornwall's coastal mining industry ended with frustration and disappointment, but with its pride intact. In a world where national and trans-national economies dictate agendas, Cornish deep mining may seem just another victim of market forces, but

the effect that the loss of the industry had on the local economy, and on its culture, was devastating.

Mining was always gruelling work. Even in the surface works of modern tin mines, amidst the streaming torrents of rust-red water and the rattle of machinery, chill air seeped into the bones. The fisherman in a gale of wind, the farmer struggling with rock-bound fields have the open sky above them. Miners worked through heatwave and hurricane in their own underworld.

There is a sweetness in the atmosphere of mines. It is a mix of deoxygenated air and the odour of mud and murky water. Daylight fades fast from the mouths of adit or shaft. Within yards it dims to a watery haze until fading totally, to where only headlamps sift through the gloom. The colours of the surrounding

Above
Boats at Sennen.
Simon Cook.

Opposite page
Hard rock mining.
Ashley Peters.

rock are ochre and dense grey shot through with sparks of fiery orange and with the ghostly fluorescence of lichens here and there. Below ground is a landscape in its own right.

The ingenuity of Cornish miners and engineers was exceptional. The industry saw great advances in technology during the Age of Steam and the genius of such men as Richard Trevithick was of world significance. The social consequences of 19th century mining were not so positive, however. This was a heavy industry within a hostile environment and conditions in the 19th century coastal mines were grim. Women and young boys toiled with heavy hammers and long-handled shovels amidst the heaps of broken rock; they scraped raw arsenic from reeking labyrinths on whose walls the arsenic had crystallized after tin ore was roasted in calciners. Arsenic was a lucrative by-product of mineral mining that sustained the industry when tin prices were low. It was used in other industries and as a pesticide on the American cotton fields. At Botallack and in the Kenidjack Valley, the atmospheric ruins of arsenic calciners fascinate us today. The reality, even in the early years of the 20th century was that workers were barely protected against such lethal toxicity. There is not much

'Heritage' to be proud of in the brutalising work that reduced a community's health and that sapped the energies of entire generations. Nor is there much to cherish in the Cornish diaspora that saw thousands of miners and their families forced into economic migration.

Today, the end of deep mining on the Land's End Peninsula is all the more shocking because it seems to be irreversible. If all those years of hard work and sacrifice had any lasting justification it was that the industry might have had a viable future. Yet there is little hope even in the search for mining work abroad, the traditional last resort of the hard rock miner.

The future of what is left of hard rock mining on the Land's End Peninsula seems to lie with tourism, an industry which itself has a long pedigree in West Cornwall. From early in the nineteenth century 'visitors' from outside Cornwall were sustaining a number of coastal resorts and by mid-century the Victorian fashion for popular holidaymaking came to West Cornwall with the extension of the railway to the far west. By the beginning of the 20th century, Land's End was drawing thousands of tourists who seemed to be obsessed with the compulsion of simply

reaching this 'farre point'. Newlyn and St Ives attracted their legendary painters and the transformation of St Ives from fishing port to holiday resort became inevitable.

In many ways tourism is a traditional industry in West Cornwall. It has passed through structural changes in the same way as farming, fishing and mining have. Tourism has a future within the rural landscape, because of initiatives such as farm diversification, the funding of innovative small businesses and projects such as the development of Geevor Mine as a tourism and leisure resource. Keynote institutions such as the Tate Gallery, St Ives, the Newlyn Gallery and Penzance's Penlee House Art Gallery & Museum, sustain the area's substantial art tourism; art in West Cornwall has always been firmly rooted in the portrayal and interpretation of the landscape.

The formidable list of environmental and protective designations attached to the landscape of West Cornwall reflects the global importance of that landscape. Such recognition also encourages and sustains tourism, and while tourism might seem to have no physical continuity with the crafts and industries of the past, it is an authentic trade that exploits the resources of the landscape as much as mining, fishing and farming ever did. Today's tourism may employ a Cornish generation that has little immediate experience of the traditional work and lifestyle that they now extol and interpret, but tourism is rooted ultimately in a Cornish sense of place and in Cornish tradition.

The old structures of life in West Cornwall are changing and are being redefined inescapably by changes in the larger world. It has always been thus, even in Neolithic times, although today change is far more rapid and unpredictable. The people of West Cornwall are better equipped than ever to cope with change and to redefine their lives with imagination. For many Cornish people there is a bittersweet irony in the way that the landscape of West Cornwall is being recognised as worthy of preservation and protection while so much of the work that shaped it is in decline or is defunct. Yet cherishing that landscape seems entirely logical. It is still a resource and a work place as much as a thing of beauty. The challenge for the future is how best to preserve this beautiful landscape, while securing a fruitful life for those who live upon it, in a world where old values and new opportunities are not incompatible.

"The people of West Cornwall are better equipped than ever to cope with change and to redefine their lives with imagination"

The Author

Des Hannigan is a writer and photographer who lives at Morvah on the north coast of the Land's End Peninsula. He writes travel guides for publishers such as *Lonely Planet* and *AA Publishing* and has written guides to Britain, Ireland, Northern Europe, Greece, Spain and North Pakistan. During the 1980s he worked as a reporter for several newspapers including *The Cornishman*, *The St Ives Times & Echo* and the Plymouth-based *Sunday Independent*. Over the years he has been a regular contributor to Penwith District Council's many successful Tourism initiatives. His local work includes National Trust publications, guidebooks to rock climbing on the Land's End Peninsula's sea cliffs and a collection of topographical and wildlife essays, *Impressions of a Landscape* (St Ives Printing & Publishing Co., 1988) that was based on the popular series *Coast & Country*, first published in The Cornishman, Western Morning News and Cornish Life magazine. Much of the inspiration for the text of *Atlantic Edge* derives from the Coast & Country series.

Acknowledgements

Des Hannigan wishes to thank the following for their advice and support in the production of this book; Mike Foxley of Penwith District Council for his unflagging enthusiasm and professionalism and John Lindfeld and Mike Rosendale for making the original *Atlantic Edge* a pleasure to work on.

Special thanks to Richard Vanhinsbergh of *The Cornishman*, David Clarke of *Cornish Life* and Geoff Carver and Toni Carver of *The St Ives Times & Echo*; archaeologists Adam Sharpe and Jackie Nowakowski whose professional work, and that of their colleagues of the Cornwall Archaeological Unit, represents the authentic interpretation of the ancient landscape; the National Trust and the Cornwall Wildlife Trust for invaluable biological information and advice; Dr Stan Salmon of the University of Derby, and current President of the Royal Geological Society of Cornwall, for advice on Geology over many years.

Acknowledgement of the best of all sources on West Cornwall, the works of John Thomas Blight, Peter A. S. Pool and Charles Thomas.

Grateful thanks especially to the many outstanding photographers for illuminating the pages of the original edition and of this edition.

Thanks above all to my many friends and associates in farming, fishing and mining. They know the Cornish landscape inside and out.

Previous page
The Crowns, Botallack.
Philip Trevennen.

Left
The Brisons, Cape Cornwall.
Bob Berry.

Further Reading

Blight, J. T: *A Week at the Land's End* (1861), (This edition, Alison Hodge, 1989).

Cooke, Ian McNeil: *Mermaid to Merrymaid; Journey to the Stones* (1987 & 1996).

Deacon, Bernard, and George, Andrew, and Perry, Ronald: *Cornwall at the Crossroads?* (CoSERG, 1988).

Folliott Stokes: *From Land's End to the Lizard* (1909).

Hudson, W. H: *The Land's End* (1908) (This edition Wildwood House, 1981).

Jenkin, A. K. Hamilton: *Cornwall And Its People* (David & Charles Reprints, 1970).

Maber, Richard and Tregoning, Angela (edited by): *Kilvert's Cornish Diary* (Alison Hodge, 1989).

Paton, Jean A: *Wild Flowers in Cornwall and the Isles of Scilly* (D. Bradford Barton, 1968).

Payton, Philip: *Cornwall: A History* (Cornwall Editions, 1996/2004).

Phillips, Roy: *Cornwall Seasons* (Halsgrove, 2002).

Pye-Smith, Charlie: *In Search of Neptune* (The National Trust, 1990).

Sagar-Fenton, Michael: *Penlee, The Loss of a Lifeboat* (Truran, 1991).

Sharpe, Adam: *St Just, An Archaeological Survey of the Mining District.*

Soulsby, Ian: *A History of Cornwall* (Phillimore, 1986).

Stevens, James: *A Cornish Farmer's Diary* (Edited and published by P.A.S. Pool, 1977).

Symons, Alison: *Tremedda Days* (Tabb House, 1992).

Weatherhill, Craig: *Belerion: Ancient Sites of Land's End* (Alison Hodge, 1981).

Williams, Douglas: *Mounts Bay* (Bossiney Books, 1984) and *Around Newlyn, Mousehole and Penzance* (Bossiney Books, 1988).

Contact Details

PHOTOGRAPHERS

Liam Addison	**www.liamaddison.co.uk**
Bob Berry	**www.bbphoto.net**
Simon Cook	**www.cornish-images.com**
Ander Gunn	**(01736) 350596**
Tim Guthrie	**www.tim@timguthrie.co.uk**
Des Hannigan	**(01736) 788643**
Rob Jewell	**www.rjphoto.co.uk**
Ian Kingsnorth	**www.lephoto.com**
Joe Lewis	**(01736) 788897**
Steve Martin	**(01736) 794837**
Ashley Peters	**(01736) 763171**
Andrew Ray	**www.andrewrayphotography.com**
Adam Sharpe	**(01736) 787836**
Philip Trevennen	**www.trevennen.com**
Paul Watts/VisitCornwall	**www.imageclick.co.uk**

PRODUCTION

Penwith District Council	**www.penwith.gov.uk**
Design & Print	**www.designp.co.uk**